Healthy Children, Healthy Minds

Healthy Children, Healthy Minds

Helping Children Succeed NOW for a Brighter Future

Marcel Lebrun and Kimberly Williams

ROWMAN & LITTLEFIELD EDUCATION
A division of
ROWMAN & LITTLEFIELD
Lanham • Boulder • New York • Toronto • Plymouth, UK

Published by Rowman & Littlefield Education
A division of Rowman & Littlefield
4501 Forbes Boulevard, Suite 200, Lanham, Maryland 20706
www.rowman.com

10 Thornbury Road, Plymouth PL6 7PP, United Kingdom

British Library Cataloguing in Publication Information Available

Library of Congress Cataloging-in-Publication Data

Lebrun, Marcel, 1957-
Healthy children, healthy minds : helping children succeed NOW for a brighter future / Marcel Lebrun and Kimberly Williams.
p. cm.
Includes bibliographical references.
ISBN 978-1-61048-925-6 (cloth : alk. paper) -- ISBN 978-1-61048-926-3 (pbk. : alk. paper) -- ISBN 978-1-61048-927-0 (electronic)
1. Child mental health. 2. Brain--Care and hygiene. 3. Mental health education. 4. Mental health promotion. 5. Children--Health and hygiene. 6. Health promotion. I. Title.
RJ499.L356 2014
618.92'89--dc23   2014004835

∞™ The paper used in this publication meets the minimum requirements of American National Standard for Information Sciences Permanence of Paper for Printed Library Materials, ANSI/NISO Z39.48-1992.

Printed in the United States of America

I would like to dedicate this book to my partner, Carl, who continually encourages and supports me every day. His ongoing commitment to my success is truly appreciated. Having you in my life helps me to attain new heights of creativity, personal growth, and achievement. (Marcel Lebrun)

To my family—I am blessed to have loved ones in my life who continue to unconditionally love and support me through the long hours of working to make the world a better, safer, more mindful, caring place for all. (Kimberly Williams)

Contents

Preface

"Education makes better minds, and knowledge of the mind can make better education."

—Daniel Willingham

What can be more important to the future of humanity than helping our next generation develop their minds in healthy ways? This book provides a wake-up call for adults to focus our attention on what really matters—creating healthy children with healthy minds. We must cultivate healthy minds that are thoughtful, focused on their own and others' mental, physical, and spiritual health, as well as the health of other living creatures and of the environment locally and around the world. We must purposefully cultivate minds that work to improve the welfare of all citizens of the world. At the same time, we all want to see children happily playing outdoors, making friends, eating healthy food, and having purpose, drive, motivation, and exuding the qualities of honesty and integrity.

Instead we are currently bombarded with images of children who are dishonest and lack integrity—who are self-absorbed, who abuse their bodies. Somewhere during the past several decades there has been a complete shift in the moral, physical, intellectual, and emotional capabilities of American children—or at least the ones portrayed in the popular culture.

The twenty-first-century generation of children and adolescents is riddled with psychological, behavioral, and socio-emotional problems and challenges. The Centers for Disease Control and Prevention reported that prescription drug use among our nation's children has risen steadily since 1999 and continues to rise (CDC, 2010). The number of children and adolescents who are on medication, failing at school, and in our juvenile prison system is staggering. The increase in youth violence and incarceration has increased tenfold since the 1950–1960's.

Researchers have been overwhelmed with the amount of data that has been collected on dysfunctional children and adolescents. Failing schools have contributed to failing students. The breakdown of the family and lack of parental support has contributed to growing numbers of depressed, suicidal, anxious, confused, and fundamentally troubled youth. The educational and family systems have failed to keep up with the societal changes and failed to make accommodations to this ever-growing population of disenfranchised and disillusioned youth.

The purpose of this book is to regain the energy that is needed to meet the needs of all children—in America and around the world. We need an ongoing campaign for all educators, adults, and citizens to take responsibility to raise healthy, mindful children of the 21st century. The roles and responsibilities of the present adult generation are to provide safe and healthy environments for all children to develop healthy bodies and healthy minds, so they can contribute in positive ways to the global community. The models adults present to children make lasting impressions during the formative years. Children watch adult role models in the media, at home, in their communities, and at school, and try to emulate them, thus influencing their own later adult behaviors.

What are adults showing children by their behaviors? Are adults inadvertently creating a generation of dysfunctional and egotistical youth that will only care about their own immediate needs and not an iota about anyone else? Will American adults create a generation of self-absorbed monsters who are focused only on their own survival, thus reverting back to the days of the caveman where only the strongest of the species survived? If this does occur in the next generation, America will be a place where its citizens attempt to survive in any way they can, and our environment may not survive.

We the authors are motivated to stop that wave of dysfunction and future destruction. We believe that we adults can and must purposefully work with children to help them develop in healthy and mindful ways. There are solutions and interventions available to direct children and youth in the right direction. The situation is not hopeless. The goal of this book is to help all educators and other adults who work with children to use these strategies to shape the minds of future generations, by modeling healthy behavior and encouraging and showing children how to be healthy and mindful, so that they can become positive, caring citizens of the world, ones who contribute to make the world a place that is healthy, mindful, caring, and productive.

This book is set up around three major themes. The first theme, covered in part I is Keeping the Brain and Mind Healthy. Chapter 1 will focus on the critical role of exercise for the healthy and developing mind. Chapter 2 will focus on nutrition. Chapter 3 will focus on the arts as providing necessary stimulation for the young mind. Chapter 4 will focus on language development and mathematical computing and the brain and mind.

The second major theme will be discussed in part II: Challenges to Brain and Mind Health. In this part we discuss attention issues and problems, multitasking, brain injuries and brain damage, substance abuse, physical illness, obesity, mental illness, and violence and abuse.

The third theme presented in part III shares strategies for building a healthy brain and mind. Specifically we will provide hands-on strategies for purposeful cultivation of mindfulness and meditation, strategies for purposeful thinking, increasing awareness of emotional states, and creating healthy lifestyles and social relations, and alternative therapies.

Each chapter will be structured using the acronym NOW. Because we believe that not only is now the time to do something about it, but part of mindfulness is focusing on the present "NOW." Using this acronym each chapter will be structured to examine the *Nature of the issue and how it affects children*. Then the chapter will focus on *Ongoing strategies to improve the issue/problem—how can we make this better?* And finally: *What can you do right now?*

We recognize that as parents and teachers, you are bombarded with information. This book pulls from the best sources of information and critiques the theories and evidence. Our goal is to provide hands-on strategies that can help turn the tide of problematic, ultimately self-harming behavior that is happening in our culture to create a better place for us all to live.

Part I

Keeping the Brain and Mind Healthy

Chapter One

Exercise: The Mind on the Move

One of the most important life lessons for children to learn for the health of their bodies and minds is the necessity of regular exercise. The evidence is consistent and powerful—exercise is essential and one of the most important things all people can do for a healthy body and healthy brain and mind. We start with this chapter for this reason—if you get no farther in this book and learn only to get and keep children moving, you will have learned one of the most important lessons for a healthy brain and mind. How much and what kind of exercise is enough? How do we know? How can we encourage children to exercise enough for their body and brain development?

NATURE OF THE ISSUE AND HOW IT AFFECTS CHILDREN

According to a report in *Medical News Today*, "Less than 50% of primary school-aged boys and under 28% of girls reach the minimum levels of exercise necessary to maintain proper health" (Fitzgerald, 2013, para 1). Child and adult obesity in the United States is reaching epidemic proportions. Our health care costs are rising as a result of the major physical illnesses that result.

In today's video and computer game and television and media culture, children have become more sedentary in their free time. Even in school, the amount of time devoted to physical activity in physical education classes or recess has declined as greater accountability measures in the form of state testing and local, state, and federal mandates have increased. In an effort to increase instructional time, children have far less time for physical play.

In addition, sports budgets have been dismantled in schools. So what happens to children? They spend most of their days sitting down. They get almost no exercise each day. Their bodies are not strong. Their hearts are not strong. Their brains are not as strong as they could be. They are out of shape and at much greater risk of childhood obesity and other health problems such as diabetes, heart disease, and so on. Studies have found that type two diabetes in children increases their risk for heart and kidney disease and hypertension.

Alarming rates of memory issues and Attention Deficit Hyperactivity diagnoses have led researchers to examine non-drug options to treatment. A study conducted by Bucci and his colleagues and published in *Neuroscience* found that "Observations of ADHD children in Vermont summer camps revealed that athletes or team sports players tended to display a better response to behavioral interventions than children who were more sedentary" (Rattue, 2013).

Bucci stated in an interview in "Medical News Today" that

> "the implication is that exercising during development, as your brain is growing, is changing the brain in concert with normal developmental changes, resulting in your having more permanent wiring of the brain in support of things like learning and memory. It seems important to [exercise] early in life" (Rattue, 2013).

Exercise can help with stabilizing moods and may be useful for adolescents as they go through puberty to help with the mood swings they experience. Exercise has been shown to improve memory, improve mood, reduce stress, improve cognitive functioning, and improve overall health. It seems preposterous that something so crucial to our health and well-being and could be so helpful in improving learning and memory is being shut out of our schools—ironically for the sake of learning.

ONGOING STRATEGIES TO IMPROVE THE ISSUE—HOW CAN WE MAKE THIS BETTER?

The U.S. Department of Agriculture recommends that children and adolescents between the ages of six and seventeen every day should get an hour or more of "moderate or vigorous intensity aerobic physical activity . . . and as a part of their 60 or more minutes children and adolescents should include muscle-strengthening activities like climbing . . . at least 3 days a week." Also three days a week should include very vigorous activity for sixty minutes—like running (How Much Physical Activity Is Needed, para. 3). The Centers for Disease Control and Prevention have the same guidelines and suggestions. They break down the nature of the activity into the following categories:

1. Aerobic activity (sixty minutes each day)—they suggest that three days should be high intensity aerobic activity.
2. Muscle strengthening (at least three days a week and can be part of the sixty minutes per week)—they suggest activities like push-ups, but weightlifting with weights, lunges, squats, sit ups, etc. are also helpful.
3. Bone strengthening for three days a week as part of the sixty minutes per day. The CDC recommends activities like running or jump rope. Any jumping activities like trampoline play (be careful since there are many accidents on trampolines, but children if careful enjoy and can get great exercise on them).

Children and adolescents may think they are working hard, but using a 10-point scale of "perceived exertion" may help. The goal is to try to get them to get their heart rates up to the point where they feel like they are working moderately hard (5–6 on a scale of 1–10 where 10 is the absolute maximum physical exertion a child can do) to very hard (8–9) for part of the time. That is, children need to learn to push themselves, sometimes not only for the good health of their brains and minds, but also to help them learn that they can work hard and feel a sense of accomplishment from hard work. This persistence and hard work will hopefully carry through to learning and challenging tasks of their minds.

In a rare example of a clinical trial involving exercise and its impact on children and their learning and development, Davis and her colleagues (2011) found that their "experimental data offer evidence that a vigorous after school aerobic exercise program improved executive function . . . among overweight children." They also found "changes in corresponding brain activation patterns [that provided] partial support of a benefit to mathematics performance." They, like many other neuroscientists, support the notion that "executive function develops in childhood and is crucial for adaptive behavior and development" and exercise seems to improve this development.

Our ability to control our behavior and make decisions and problem solve is based on the development of our executive function areas of the cortex. This evidence supporting the key role of exercise in building executive function is incredibly important. We can make exercise fun and even build it into activities such as video-gaming that children really like to do. A study in the *Journal of Pediatrics* reported that there are some kinds of active video games that "may provide an alternative type of exercise to prevent stationary behavior in children" (Fitzgerald, 2013).

In this study on active video-gaming ("exer-gaming"), researchers used an active video console and found that participants who engaged in this activity had an "increased energy expenditure equal to moderate intensity exercise" when playing "high intensity games like the 200m hurdles on Kinect Sports." Fitzgerald references an earlier study in the archives of *Pediatrics and Adolescent Medicine* that showed that "children who played active video games burned over four times as many calories as when they were playing an inactive game." They also suggested that these high intensity games may end up encouraging children to be more active and receive the health benefits from moderate exercise.

WHAT CAN YOU DO RIGHT NOW?

Demand regular physical activity and *high quality physical education* in school. As many school districts are cutting physical education (PE) time and recess/play time, children are getting far less of the activity they need in a given week. As parents and teachers or other concerned community members, lobby for more time spent in PE courses and after-school intramural activities and organized athletics. Children should strive toward sixty minutes of physical activity per day. As most of their waking time is spent in schools, this is the logical place for this to happen.

Making exercise fun and part of the daily routine (even in bad weather) is critically important for children and adolescents. Young people need to get at least sixty minutes of cardio-vascular exercise every day. Given the very busy lives of families and young people, finding time for this kind of activity can be difficult. And this can be particularly challenging in areas where the weather can be extreme or where finding safe spaces to exercise can be difficult.

Important things to consider include the following:

- Ensure that an adult always supervises young children playing outside.
- Always use sunscreen any time a child is outside (SPF of fifty preferably).
- Ensure that there is time for free or unstructured play.
- Ensure that there is time for structured physical activities to make sure children are moving around sufficiently and pushing themselves.
- Ensure that children wear clothing appropriate for the climate.
- In cold weather climates, check for signs of frostbite on any exposed areas.
- If children must remain indoors because of the weather, find a safe place where they can be active—in a gymnasium at school, or a spot in the house where they can jog in place, do jumping jacks, and so forth. Consider having an age-appropriate workout video or music.
- Encourage "Exergaming" or "active video-gaming" for video game junkies.
- Find safe places to go for walks (parks, woods, sidewalks, and so on)—this is good for adults and children. Sometimes children need to build up

their stamina; start with shorter walks and build up to longer ones. For younger children, think of ways to make it interesting—go on a "treasure hunt" for the prettiest leaves or see how many seconds a child can run or walk like an elephant.

- Make a set time every day to exercise, and make it part of the family routine, like eating dinner. Going for an after-dinner walk can be very helpful for metabolizing this large meal.
- Consider a "tread mill desk" for older students or adults where one can walk and do work on a computer or read at the same time.
- If the weather is bad and there are no safe spaces to walk, children can carefully go up and down stairs or dance to music they enjoy or run in place or do jumping jacks to music.
- Families that play together, stay together. Encourage families to exercise together during their time together. Schools can organize family fun times that are active hikes, walks, or times to use the gym facilities.
- Just MOVE—often!

TOP TIPS FOR TEACHERS

1. Be a good role model and exercise yourself and share with your students what you do. Exercise with them!
2. Encourage students to be active and get sixty minutes of cardiovascular activity every day—ask them to report back to you what they did and how hard they worked.
3. Build in some kind of movement into the classroom—either stretching breaks, jogging in place, opportunities to walk—even walk around the halls together or outside for even 5–10 minute breaks. Students will come back more energized and their minds more focused (especially if this becomes a regular part of the school day).

REFERENCES

Davis, C., Tomporowski, P., and McDowell, J. (2011). Exercise Improves Executive Function and Achievement and Alters Brain Activation in Overweight Children: A Randomized Controlled Trial. *Health Psychology, 30*(1), 91–98.

Fitzgerald, K. (2013). Active Video Games Act as Exercise for Children. *Medical News Today: Health News.* Retrieved June 7, 2013, from http://www.medicalnewstoday.com/articles/260651.php.

How Much Physical Activity Is Needed? (n.d.). *ChooseMyPlate.gov.* Retrieved June 6, 2013, from http://www.choosemyplate.gov/physical-activity/amount.html.

Rattue, P. (2013). Exercise Affects the Brain. *Medical News Today: Health News.* Retrieved June 7, 2013, from http://www.medicalnewstoday.com/articles.

Chapter Two

Nutrition, Water, and Air: Healthy Essential Fuel for the Healthy Mind!

We all need healthy food and safe drinking water and fresh air to survive. The brain can live far longer without food than without water, and we can live only a few minutes without air. Everything we take into the body affects the body, and most everything we take in affects the brain (particularly if the substance crosses what is called the "blood-brain-barrier").

The brain needs healthy food to function and adequate water and clean air. But what exactly does this mean? What kind of healthy food do we need to provide for children to have healthy brain and mind development? How much water is required? How important is air quality? What toxins are in our environment that affect brain and mind development?

NATURE OF THE ISSUE AND HOW IT AFFECTS CHILDREN

Poor Nutrition

Poor nutrition is perhaps one of the greatest worldwide health concerns, one that will affect as many as one billion of the world's children in the future. The United Nations has reported that "malnourishment could stunt and handicap an estimated 1 billion children worldwide by 2020 unless a more focused nutrition campaign is launched" (CNN, 2000).

In addition to inadequate nutrition affecting children, poor nutrition harms the fetus in women who are malnourished. Direct links have been made between malnourishment and diseases, including chronic diseases (such as diabetes) and learning problems/deficiencies and delays. Some studies have shown that children who do not get proper nutrition are at higher risk of behavioral disorders or problems. And some recent studies have shown that those who eat a healthy breakfast perform better academically (Mahoney et al., 2005).

In the United States, a study with the U.S. Department of Agriculture and Harvard University found that U.S. children who ate fast food, compared with those who did not, consumed more total calories, more calories per gram of food, more total and saturated fat, more total carbohydrates, more added sugars and more sugar-sweetened beverages, but less milk, fiber, fruit, and non-starchy vegetables. The study also revealed out of the two days surveyed, those children who consumed fast food on only one day showed similar nutrient shortfalls on the day they had fast food. But they did not show these shortfalls on the other day (Bliss, 2004, para. 3).

Our increased reliance on fast and processed foods is resulting in a generation of poorly nourished children; some studies have estimated that daily meals from fast-food establishments have increased from 2 percent to 10 percent since the late 1970s (Bliss, 2004). One of the many concerns associated with poor nutrition, including greater reliance on fast and processed foods, is an increase in childhood obesity which will be discussed in the second section of this book.

Access to Safe Drinking Water

There have been campaigns to assure fresh, safe drinking water in schools. The EPA reports that many schools have lead in their school drinking water, even if the community water supply meets EPA regulations, due to lead plumbing and seasonal use patterns. The U.S. EPA oversees the Safe Drinking Water Act, which guarantees safe drinking water (www.epa.gov). For the good of our environment and because of new health discoveries showing the negative impact of plastic bottles, we need to promote healthy drinking water from the faucet.

Providing safe drinking water to the world's children is also a high priority for the World Health Organization and the United Nations as dehydration is a leading cause of death and other physical and learning problems in high-poverty areas of the world. The United Kingdom has instituted a program called "Water Is Cool in School" to promote providing healthy drinking water to children in school (www.wateriscoolinschool.org).

A Welsh study in which students in 275 elementary schools were provided fresh water and encouraged to drink adequate amounts of water daily found that teachers reported that they believed children's concentration was improved and that they were less tired in class. Teachers also reported that children were not drinking so many sugary fizzy drinks. Teachers felt that the children enjoyed having drinking water available, and increased the amount of water that they drank during the school day (PHS Group, 2005, para. 3).

The brain and the rest of the body need water and are comprised of mostly water. Dehydration has a detrimental effect on the brain's ability to think.

Toxins in Air, Water, Food, and the Environment

Hidden toxic dangers in the environment surround our children. One such danger is poisoning. Perhaps the most pervasive threat to the health and safety of children is lead-poisoning, although certainly children are also at risk of poisoning from other environmental and common household elements. Lead poisoning affects healthy brain development and learning and memory.

The most dangerous and widespread environmental poisoning threats that face our children (including lead, mercury, radon, and DEET) can be found in air, food, or water, as well as household products. Educators, parents, and other caregivers need to be on the lookout for hazardous substances for children and possible cognitive and/or physical effects from accidental poisoning.

Lead Poisoning

According to the Centers for Disease Control (CDC), unintentional poisoning is the fourth leading cause of injury and death for children aged fifteen to twenty-four. As the American Academy of Pediatrics (AAP) wrote, "Of all the health problems caused by the environment, lead poisoning is the most preventable. Despite this, almost 1 million children in the United States have elevated levels of lead in their blood. Any child can be at risk for lead poisoning" (2005, para. 1).

Lead poisoning has been on the decline since 1991 when the CDC reported that as many as one in eleven American children had significantly elevated lead levels. Since that time, airborne lead from the use of leaded gasoline has been virtually eliminated. Currently, much lead poisoning in children happens from lead paint in the form of dust or in the soil. Also, lead poisoning can be transferred from mother to child through the placenta and/ or breast milk, and lead can be ingested by drinking tap water from lead plumbing (AAP Policy Statement, 2005).

U.S. News & World Report (2008) stated that lead poisoning "afflicts an estimated 890,000 American preschoolers [and] can be a threat in any house or apartment with lead paint, even if fresh paint is layered over it." Children can be exposed not only through paint on houses but, as has recently been discovered, through paint on recalled toys, as well as through the following:

- soils
- household dusts

- leaded paints
- gasoline

The report features the research of Theodore Lidsky and Jay Schneider, who studied fifty children with dangerous levels of lead in their blood and found that the following are warning signs:

- fine motor skills problems
- memory problems
- concentration problems
- behavioral problems that look like attention deficit hyperactivity disorder
- reduction in IQ scores, according to some studies

Some of the signs look similar to attention deficit disorder. Adult caregivers, teachers, or anyone else working with children should encourage lead-poisoning blood tests for children. Some studies have shown that even very low levels of lead in the blood of young children can produce problematic effects like the ones listed above, as well as trouble with balance, coordination, problem solving, and movement (Schmidt 1999). There are treatment agents that can reduce lead levels in the blood. Prevention is obviously preferable— as is catching problems early in childhood.

Mercury Poisoning

A study published in 2006 showed a decline in certain kinds of neurodevelopmental disorders (such as those discussed in an earlier chapter on the brain and learning) after thimerosal (which contains mercury) was removed from childhood vaccines in the United States. Despite evidence of the harmful effects of mercury, however, it is a primary ingredient in many dental fillings (mercuryexposure.org).

And another study in 2006 in Texas showed that as environmental mercury levels increased, so did rates of autism and special education services (Palmer et al. 2006). In addition, another study has shown that mercury exposure in utero and in early childhood from eating mercury-exposed fish is linked to some deficits among children with higher mercury levels (Davidson et al., 2006).

A study conducted by D. A. Geier and M. R. Geier (2007) urine-tested seventy-one children with autism and found that these children had significantly higher (toxic) mercury levels than their siblings and other control group members. It is important to note that these studies are hotly contested and that there have been no causal links—the studies are typically correlational (showing relationships between two things), and no studies show a direct causal relationship. However, the evidence bears mentioning here so that parents and other caregivers can make informed decisions.

Pesticides

Pesticides can be found in the food we eat or the water we drink or we can be exposed through the air or skin. The AAP's position on the use of insect repellents containing DEET (N,N-diethyl-m-toluamide, also known as N,N-diethyl-3-methylbenzamide) on children is as follows: DEET-containing products are the most effective mosquito repellents available. DEET also is effective as a repellent against a variety of other insects, including ticks. It should be used when there is a need to prevent insect-borne disease. The concentration of DEET in products may range from less than 10 percent to over 30 percent. The efficacy of DEET plateaus at a concentration of 30 percent, the maximum concentration currently recommended for infants and children.

The major difference in the efficacy of products relates to their duration of action. Products with concentrations around 10 percent are effective for periods of approximately two hours. As the concentration of DEET increases, the duration of activity increases; for example, a concentration of about 24 percent has been shown to provide an average of five hours of protection (AAP, 2003, para. 2).

The AAP does not recommend using DEET products on children under the age of two months, and other organizations suggest avoiding the use of DEET products on children under two years of age. According to the Sierra Club, Canada legally banned products with more than 30 percent DEET because some research has shown that in high doses neurological problems can occur from excessive DEET exposure in rats (www.sierraclub.ca).

However, the stance among the medical community is that the benefits of avoiding diseases transmitted by biting insects from the effective use of DEET outweigh the risks.

Radon—Silent and in the Air

According to the Environmental Protection Agency (EPA), radon is responsible for an estimated fourteen thousand preventable lung cancer deaths per year (with estimates ranging between seven thousand and thirty thousand) (EPA 2008). The EPA states, "Radon is a cancer-causing natural radioactive gas that you can't see, smell, or taste. Its presence in your home can pose a danger to your family's health. Radon is the leading cause of lung cancer among non-smokers. Radon is the second leading cause of lung cancer in America and claims about 20,000 lives annually" (2008, para. 1).

The EPA encourages families to test their homes for radon. Schools should also test for radon and provide education to families to promote testing (perhaps raising money to assist low-income families). January is the designated National Radon Awareness/Action Month, and states are encouraged to promote educational campaigns. Drinking water can also carry radon and should be tested.

Other Household Chemicals and Poisons

An article about childhood poisoning by Hingley (1996) states, "Iron containing products remain the biggest problem by far when it comes to childhood poisoning. Most people regard their home as a safe haven, a calming oasis in a stormy world. But home can be a dangerous place when it comes to accidental poisoning, especially accidental poisoning of children. One tablet of some medicines can wreak havoc on or kill a child."

Some of the other non-pharmacological substances that the American Association of Poison Control Centers reported were

- glues
- alcohols (ethanol, isopropanol, methanol)
- art supplies
- batteries
- automotive/boat products (e.g., ethylene glycol)
- building products
- other chemicals (acids, acetone, pool products, cleaning solvents/chemicals, cosmetics)
- fertilizers/herbicides/insecticides
- gases
- paints/varnishes
- plants
- stings
- tobacco products

Pharmaceutical Substances

The following commonly found elements in medicine cabinets were among the most responsible for pediatric poisonings:

- analgesics (aspirin, acetaminophen, ibuprofen)
- analgesics with other narcotic substances such as codeine, oxycodone, and so forth
- topical anesthetics
- antianxiety agents

- antidepressants
- antihistamines
- antimicrobials (e.g., antibiotics)
- cold medications
- sedatives
- stimulants/street drugs
- vitamins (including iron and fluoride)

Many adults may consider drugs such as aspirin, acetaminophen, and ibuprofen to be relatively benign, but the truth is they are among the drugs most commonly associated with overdose deaths (often in cases of suicide) and toxic levels brought to emergency rooms. We must be especially careful with these common household substances to be sure caps are on tightly and that they are out of reach of children.

ONGOING STRATEGIES TO IMPROVE THE ISSUE—HOW CAN WE MAKE THIS BETTER?

Healthy Diet at Home

Children need to eat healthy food. The guidelines are available on the updated food pyramid (promoted by the U.S. Department of Agriculture). An individualized "pyramid," or plan, depends on age, gender, weight, and physical activity level. To create an individualized plan for a child or children, visit the U.S. Department of Agriculture at www.mypyramid.gov for more information.

For example, for the typically developing eight-year-old female who gets less than thirty minutes of physical exercise, the plan is for fourteen hundred calories per day: 5 ounces of grains (preferably whole grains), 1.5 cups of vegetables, 1.5 cups of fruits, 2 cups of milk, and 4 ounces of meat and beans.

The information on the website promotes at least sixty minutes of physical activity every day, limiting oils to less than four tablespoons per day. Extra fats and sugars should be limited to 170 calories or less, with the following variation in the veggies: 1.5 cups of dark green/leafy vegetables weekly, 1 cup of orange vegetables, 1 cup of dry beans and peas weekly, 2.5 cups of starchy vegetables, and 4.5 cups of other vegetables, all at least weekly. More information can be found on the U.S. Department of Agriculture's website at www.mypyramid.gov.

Healthy Diet at School: School Breakfast and Lunch Programs

As school-aged children spend much of their waking hours in school, schools have become places where low-income children are consistently able to receive free or reduced-price lunches and breakfasts.

Mahoney and associates found that children who took advantage of the school breakfast program had improved academic performance in school. School lunches and breakfasts in low-income areas are still often highly processed; were they made even more nutritious, they would likely yield even greater cognitive and physical results.

Another concern about children eligible for school lunches is the lack of healthy food available to children on the weekends and during school vacations. Communities need to work together to ensure proper nutrition is made available to all children every day.

There have been some strides made as greater attention is being paid to school breakfasts and lunches and their nutritional value. However, some school nutrition experts have shown some concern because of the increased amount of food waste that resulted. The change to healthier more nutritious food takes time. The brain tells the body it wants more simple carbohydrates because early in human survival this was advantageous. Eating processed and/or simple carbohydrates that have high levels of sugar or sweetener is problematic.

The Food Rules

Changing to healthier eating habits (or as Michael Pollan strongly urges in his "Food Rules") "Eat food." Simply put, he wants people to eat food mostly from plants and in smaller quantities. He argues that we should not eat food with many ingredients that "your great-grandmother wouldn't recognize as food." He provides compelling reasons to avoid heavily processed packaged food (food that will not rot eventually) that "go beyond the various chemical additives and corn and soy derivatives they contain, or the plastics in which they are typically packaged, some of which are probably toxic.

Today, Pollan shows that foods are "processed in such ways specifically designed to get us to buy and eat more by pushing our evolutionary buttons—our inborn preferences for sweetness and fat and salt" (Pollan, 2009 p. 8). There are sixty-four food rules that Pollan suggests—most of which are consistent with the Food Pyramid that the US Department of Agriculture recommends. He argues for the importance of eating colorful (natural) foods from nature and eating more like an omnivore and eating less. His rules are also relevant for children at home or at school. Healthy food for healthy developing brain and mind!

Demand Clean Drinking Water and Nutritious Food for All Children

We need to protect our environment and work together to reduce contaminants put into the ground water and other water sources. We also need to work with authorities to test and provide clean drinking water in schools and homes—and we need to be particularly vigilant in low-income areas. Also, we need to continue to fund and work to improve the quality of food provided through such programs as the federal free and reduced-price lunch and breakfast programs, as well as to assure all children access to healthy foods consistent with their individual needs.

Test Drinking Water and See How Much Kids Are Drinking

First, test your school's water fountains to determine the water's quality—test for lead and other pathogens. Determine if the drinking water is safe—if not, work with the EPA to be sure that your school offers quality water. Also, test drinking water in the homes within a community. After launching campaigns for fresh, clean water and promoting sufficient drinking of water, retest the water at various locations and different times to ensure that it is still safe. Also, observe children and ask teachers how much children are actually drinking.

Depending on size, weight, physical activity, and the weather, children should drink as many as eight to ten glasses of water per day. Suffice it to say, very few children drink that much water, and many are dehydrated in schools. The brain needs sufficient water to function effectively, and children need to be encouraged to drink more water, and they should have safe water close and available.

Clean Air. Learn Your Toxins

Adult caregivers, physicians, emergency medical personnel (e.g., first responders and EMTs), teachers, child-care workers, school administrators, and counselors should all be educated about the cognitive and physical signs of environmental poisoning, such as that due to lead or other household medications or items (more on psychoactive medications will be discussed in a later chapter).

Schools are the logical places for community-awareness campaigns about the impact of lead and other environmental toxins. Also, hospitals or community medical centers can work with communities and their members to highlight the signs of environmental toxins and to offer free lead-screening programs.

Education and screening will help, but considering the possibility of poisoning when a child shows signs of cognitive shortcomings will also help with the diagnosis—which means those on the front lines of a child's cognitive development (e.g., teachers and parents) need to be aware of the warning signs.

Lead poisoning. Consider the following recommendations to reduce risk of lead poisoning among children:

- Educate parents, teachers, and other caregivers that lead poisoning can be invisible and can harm children when they put dust or toys in their mouths.
- Ask parents and school personnel to do an inventory of possibly hazardous, lead containing material around the house.

The Department of Health can do assessments at schools or homes where lead hazards are thought to exist.

- School personnel, physicians, and parents should know the laws about universal screening—and eligibility for screening under Medicare.
- Early lead screening should ideally take place when a child is one year old—and those at higher risk should be tested again at age two.
- Parents should consider their own exposure to lead to determine if they (particularly mothers) can pass along lead poisoning to their infants.
- The Department of Housing and Urban Development does have funds to improve old homes with substantial lead paint threats.

The AAP recommends the following prevention strategies:

- Environmental lead-based threat prevention strategy
- Paint identify and abate
- Dust wet mop (assuming abatement)
- Soil—restrict play in area, plan ground cover, wash hands frequently
- Drinking water—flush cold-water pipes by running the water until it becomes as cold as it will get (a few seconds to two minutes or more). Use cold water for cooking and drinking (AAP, 2005, table 3).

The AAP also recommends avoiding any possible folk remedies, cosmetics, toys, or mineral substances that have lead in them. In addition, if parents have jobs or hobbies where they come into contact with lead, they need to be careful with their work clothing (remove it at work and wash separately, and store hobby items carefully).

Radon Testing

The EPA calls the radon threat a "health hazard with a simple solution" (EPA 2008). We know that radon is a carcinogen. We know that some homes have dangerous levels of radon. We do not know which homes unless they have been tested. There are do-it-yourself home test kits, or you can have your home professionally tested. If excessive levels are found, radon-abatement programs can be installed to reduce the levels of radon in the home. The EPA has a website where you can check your risk by state at www.epa.gov/radon/zonemap.html# more%20about%20the%20map.

Other Poisonings, Radon, and DEET

Educate yourself and your community about the need to take precautions to protect children from toxic substances in the home as well as the importance of having your home tested for radon. As far as using DEET, use as needed with percentages less than 30 percent with children older than age two.

Educational campaigns set forth by day care providers, preschool centers, and schools can be really useful for increasing awareness on these topics—as can public service announcements on television or radio. Educating children on the dangers of radon, for example, in the same way we educate them about the dangers of smoking, can be effective as well.

Environmental Threats for Children Around the World

According to the United Nations Environmental Program (UNEP), children around the world are at risk in utero, after they are born, and throughout their lives from a variety of environmental threats, such as lack of safe water and sanitation, chemical pollution and radiation, indoor and outdoor air pollution, and natural resource degradation. While some parts of the world have greater risks than others, we must work together in our global community to improve these threatening conditions.

WHAT YOU CAN DO RIGHT NOW

Some areas of the world have greater concerns about clean air than others (same with water). However, clean air and water and healthy food is important for everyone.

Food

Set a good example: Eat healthy foods and provide them in the home and classroom. Also drink water regularly and model the importance for children. See where your food comes from. If possible take children to a working farm to see where their food comes from (or can come from) and encourage them to ask questions about what they eat. As children become more mindful (as will be discussed in chapter 12) they may naturally become more inquisitive about such matters and pay closer attention to what they eat and take their time eating and savoring it.

Encourage your school to provide healthy food for all children. For poor children on free and reduced lunch and breakfast programs, school food is the healthiest food they consume sometimes. Consider examining information on the Center for Ecoliteracy's Rethinking School Lunch Guide at http://www.ecoliteracy.org/downloads/rethinking-school-lunch-guide as a starting point. There are other programs such as the National Farm to School Network at www.farmtoschool.org and the Center for Science in the Public Interest which has a downloadable "School Foods Tool Kit" on its website at http://www.cspinet.org/nutritionpolicy/ImproveSchoolFoods.html.

Water

Encourage children from the time they are very young to drink water rather than sodas or even juices—water should be the "go to" drink when thirsty and they should drink it frequently throughout the day. Make sure the water children drink is safe from toxins or environmental dangers. Try to avoid bottled water unless there is no safe drinking water available from the tap.

Air

We must be involved in the overall quality of our air, water, and earth in general for our children. UNEP has some recommendations and programs with some demonstrated successes (these are too numerous to mention here, but they can be found on their website at www.UNEP.org). For example, they recommend starting with a "climate-friendly lifestyle" that seeks to "kick the CO_2 habit," suggesting that we can make a difference and improve our planet for its future inhabitants.

Toxins

As a parent or caregiver, educate yourself about the impact of these toxic chemicals on your own and your growing child's body and brain. Be sure to work with a physician to have children screened as early as possible, and be aware of cognitive delays.

As a school teacher, administrator, or counselor, if you notice any of the warning signs, like cognitive delays or other signs, be sure to encourage the child's parents to seek medical attention as soon as possible, which should include a blood test to screen for toxic agents such as lead or mercury.

As a physician or other health care professional, conduct assessments of risk for lead and mercury poisoning. Urge parents to have their young children screened, and rule out poisoning when presented with cognitive or other constellations of symptoms that indicate possible poisoning.

TOP 3 TIPS FOR TEACHERS

1. Make sure the drinking water in your school (at fountains and sinks) and air quality is healthy (you can enlist students to help you with this task as part of a science project).
2. Encourage all students to keep and use regularly healthy, clean water bottles.
3. Teach children about healthy food and why it is so important to eat healthy and ask them to monitor their eating habits regularly (and teach by example).

REFERENCES

American Academy of Pediatrics (AAP) (2005). Policy statement: Lead exposure in children: Prevention, detection and management. Pediatrics 116 (4): 1036–46.

American Academy of Pediatrics (AAP). Patient Education Online (2008). Lead screening for children. AAP Patient Education Online. http://patiented.aap.org/content.aspx?aid=5568 (accessed June 6, 2008).

Bliss, R. M. (2004). Survey links fast food, poor nutrition among U.S. children. U.S. Department of Agriculture Research Service. www.ars.usda.gov/is/pr/2004/040105.htm (accessed June 12, 2008).CNN (2000). U.N.: Poor nutrition could handicap 1 billion children. CNN. March 20. http://archives.cnn.com/2000/WORLD/europe/03/20/nutrition.report (accessed June 12, 2008).

Davidson, P., Myers, G., Weiss, B., Shamlaye, C., and Cox, C. (2006). Prenatal methyl mercury exposure from fish consumption and child development: A review of evidence and perspectives from the Seychelles Child Development Study. Neurotoxicology 27 (6): 1106–1109.

Environmental Protection Agency. (2008). Radon. EPA. www.EPA.gov/radon (accessed October 22, 2008).

Freedman, D. S., Khan, L. K., and Dietz, W. H. (2001). Relationship of childhood obesity to coronary heart disease risk factors in adulthood: The Bogalusa heart study. Pediatrics108: 712–18.

Gable, S., Chang, Y., and Krull, J. L. (2007). Television watching and frequency of family meals are predictive of overweight onset and persistence in a national sample of school-aged children. Journal of the American Diatetic Assocation 107 (1): 53–61.

Geier, D. A., Geier, M. R. (2007). A prospective study of mercury toxicity biomarkers in autistic spectrum disorders. Journal of Toxicology and Environmental Health, Part A 70(20): 1723–30.

Hingley, A. T. (1996). Preventing childhood poisoning: Iron-containing products remain the biggest problem by far when it comes to childhood poisoning. BNET. http://findarticles.com/p/articles/mi_m1370/is_n2_v30/ai_18175435?tag=content;col1.

Kozol, Jonathan (2006). Shame of the nation: The restoration of apartheid schools in America. New York: Random House.

Mahoney, C. R., Taylor, H. A., Kanarek, R. B., and Samuel, P. (2005). Effect of breakfast composition on cognitive processes in elementary schoolchildren. Psychology and Behavior 85: 635–45.

Mayo Clinic. (2008). Childhood obesity. MayoClinic.com. www.mayoclinic.com/health/childhood-obesity/DS00698.

Palmer, R. F., Blanchard, S., Stein, Z., Mandell, D., and Miller, C. (2006). Environmental mercury release, special education rates, and autism disorder: An ecological study of Texas. Health and Place 12 (2): 203–209.

PHS Group. (2005). Drinking water provision boosts brainpower in Welsh primary schools. PHS Waterlogic. www.phs.co.uk/waterlogic/1444.html.

Pollan, M. (2009). *Food rules: An eater's manual*. New York: Penguin Books.

Schmidt, C. W. (1999). Poisoning young minds. Environmental Health Perspectives 107 (6). www.ehponline.org/docs/1999/107-6/focus.html.

Sierra Club of Canada. DEET fact sheet. Sierra Club of Canada. www.sierraclub.ca/atlantic/programs/healthycommunities/pesticides/factsheets/deet.pdf (accessed June 8, 2013).

U.S. News and World Report. 2008. Health tip: Get children tested for lead poisoning. U.S. News and World Report Online. www.usnews.com/usnews/health/healthday/080104/health-tip-get-children-tested-for lead-poisoning.htm (accessed October 22, 2008).

Chapter Three

Arts: Stimulation for the Developing Mind

INTRODUCTION

George Bernard Shaw suggested that we use a mirror to see our face and the arts to see our soul.

The creative arts are meant to excite, invigorate, and challenge individuals to experience new levels of visual, auditory, and kinesthetic stimulation. Who has not enjoyed a wonderful movie, ballet, symphony, and concert in their lifetime? Everyone is connected to the arts. It all begins with simple shapes and forms when a two-year-old has a crayon or pencil put within her grasp.

Expression is natural to the human spirit, community, culture, and sense of being. Art on cave walls can be traced back to cave dwellers. People need an outlet for creative expression. Children in our schools need to be able to relate to creative expression as a way to produce their knowledge and skills.

Scientists have shown that the arts (including music) increase the brain's ability to function and think more effectively. David Sousa (2010), a renowned expert in children's brain development, stated: "Certain brain areas respond only to music while others are devoted to initiating and coordinating movement from intense running to the delicate sway of the arms. Drama provokes specialized networks that focus on spoken language and stimulate emotions. Visual arts excite the internal visual processing system to recall reality or create fantasy with the same ease." There is quite a bit of evidence to suggest that our brains are wired for music and other arts. Students who participate in the arts (including music) perform consistently better in nearly all academic areas. Sousa has summarized the research on the brain and the arts and shows the positive impact of the arts on the brain and mind.

23

In public education today music, drama, and arts programs are being severely cut back or eliminated because of financial restraints and a perspective that the arts are not necessary for growth and development. These curriculums are often seen as frivolous and expensive. This is foolhardy and limits children's healthy brain and mind development.

NATURE OF THE ISSUE AND HOW IT AFFECTS CHILDREN

Arts programs are viewed as expensive and not efficient. The effects cannot be as easily measured like math and spelling on a standardized test. The leaders in education are often centered on fulfilling a margin on a budget. Robert Sylwester (1998) stated that "evidence from the brain sciences and evolutionary psychology increasingly suggests that the arts (along with such functions as language and math) play an important role in brain development and maintenance—so it's a serious matter for schools to deny children direct curricular access to the arts."

Denying students quality experiences with the arts restricts their development and learning. Students who have access to quality music or other arts programs consistently outscore students who do not—regardless of their socio-economic status. Students from high poverty areas can perhaps benefit the most from arts programs, yet they are the ones who are most likely to be denied these programs as cost-savings measures.

Having little to no exposure to the arts can create delays in cognitive development in some children. The Dana Consortium Report on the Arts and Cognition revealed in its studies a correlation with learning, the arts, and the development of the brain in children. It showed an interest in a performing art leads to a high state of motivation that produces the sustained attention necessary to improve performance and the training of attention that leads to improvement in other domains of cognition. Without this exposure children may experience areas of attention difficulty or focus.

Human beings are all wired differently. Genetic studies have begun to yield candidate genes that may help explain individual differences in interest in the arts. However, even though there are genetic differences it is key that the educational system provide the opportunity to children to experience the arts in a way that allows them to want to explore some of their talents and possible gifts. Schools that do not provide this type of curriculum are not providing a comprehensive service to their students. Many children have the genetic predisposition but without training or instruction that potential is never realized in schools without arts or families without means to supplement the arts.

Research has indicated that there are specific links that exist between high levels of music training and the ability to manipulate information in both working and long-term memory; these links extend beyond the domain of music training (Gazzanga, Asbury, & Rich, 2008). Increased working memory means increased creativity and production in the long run.

In children, there appear to be specific links between the practice of music and skills in geometrical representation, though not in other forms of numerical representation. So why is music not part of the math curriculum and instruction? Math is often taught very systematic and formulaic and could be enhanced greatly by the incorporation of music into the teaching of concepts to children so that something that may be abstract becomes concrete in nature.

Correlations exist between music training and both reading acquisition and sequence learning. One of the central predictors of early literacy, phonological awareness, is correlated with both music training and the development of a specific brain pathway. Early childhood teachers have long figured out that putting music and words together teaches literacy. It helps children make sense of what they are saying, singing, and saying. Music associated with words becomes a learning tool for enhanced brain functioning.

Training in acting appears to lead to memory improvement through the learning of general skills for manipulating semantic information. What better way to organize words than to make them come alive through a variety of characters and performances. Being able to become someone else in a play allows the child or the student to organize words and actions in a meaningful way that is both provoking and stimulating. Do we not all go to the movies? We as a population revere actors and actresses for their abilities to create characters we love, hate, fear, or admire. The ability of the brain to organize and retain that amount of information and words are both admirable and interesting.

Learning to dance by effective observation is closely related to learning by physical practice, both in the level of achievement and also the neural substrates that support the organization of complex actions. Effective observational learning may transfer to other cognitive skills. Kids just become better observers when they watch others demonstrating a skill they want to learn. The challenge is to give them many opportunities to observe, practice, and learn. Dance also serves an additional purpose of giving children much-needed cardio-vascular exercise.

Adult self-reported interest in aesthetics is related to a temperamental factor of openness, which in turn is influenced by dopamine-related genes. People feel good when they listen to excellent music, see a wonderful ballet, or take part in an intense and riveting play. Brain researchers Robert Zatorre and Valorie Salimoor (2013), both neuroscientist researchers, in a piece for the *New York Times* wrote, "More than a decade ago, our research team used brain imaging to show that music that people described as highly emotional engaged the reward system deep in their brains—activating subcortical nuclei known to be important in reward, motivation, and emotion. Subsequently we found that listening to what might be called 'peak emotional moments' in music—that moment when you feel a 'chill' of pleasure to a musical passage—causes the release of the neurotransmitter dopamine, an essential signaling molecule in the brain." Music is a part of our brain systems—including our emotional centers.

Our interests are developed early by exposure and experience. Children who do not have any experience with these forms of creative expression later on in life do not seem to value or seek out the activity. Interest must be developed in the early years. As adults we must cultivate children's innate interest in the arts and provide opportunities for ongoing development. This will help their developing brains and minds.

ONGOING STRATEGIES TO IMPROVE THE ISSUE—HOW CAN WE MAKE IT BETTER?

Ellen Booth Church (2013), an educator in early childhood, has recommended the following as a way to build a strong foundation for children in their early years. She recommends the following:

A) Learning Activities with Visual Art

- Encourage children to use their hands to manipulate clay, finger paint, weave, paint, and draw. This helps build fine motor skills—the same skills that children need to learn how to write letters and words.
- Ask children to express their feelings using color, texture, and structure. Children often use colors in their drawings and paintings to express a mood. And the textures of clay provide a perfect place to work out frustrations!
- Use art materials to observe, predict, experiment, and problem-solve. Open-ended art activities in which children have to make choices as to how to create a sculpture or picture help foster the development of these scientific thinking skills.
- Invite children to talk about their art with words and stories in order to promote language development.
- Use discussions with other children and shared experiences to shape social and emotional interaction skills. By inviting children to "title" their art, you invite them to use art as a language.
- Introduce new art materials, such as painting with feathers. This invites children to build a strong sense of success and mastery.

B) Learning Activities with Music and Movement

- Try yoga, jumping, running, and dancing games to help children develop large muscle skills, strength, balance, rhythm, and coordination.
- Use rhythmic clapping games, tip toe dances, and finger plays to develop small muscles of the hands and feet.
- Through singing repetitive songs and circle dancing games, introduce the math skills of patterning, sequencing, and counting.
- Engage children in rhyming songs and in singing word games to build the essential language learning skills of communication, listening, and speaking.
- Use music and movement to express emotions and develop autonomy and social interaction. This helps foster social and emotional development.

C) Learning Activities with Creative Drama and Storytelling

- Invite children to act out and create stories to develop vocabulary, sequencing, listening, and memory skills.
- Explore familiar fairy tales and nursery rhymes to encourage children to learn to distinguish between fantasy and reality.
- Encourage children to act out their own feelings and the feelings of others in stories and dramatic play center activities. This helps provide a greater understanding of their own feelings and those of others.
- Explore play themes with a variety of culturally diverse materials to promote multicultural awareness.
- Invite children to express a "story" with their bodies. This provides opportunities for children to develop body awareness.

WHAT CAN YOU DO NOW?

1. Enhance exposure to the arts for enhanced cognitive growth and development.
2. Integrate music listening as part of the core curriculum and use it to differentiate instruction
3. Creating music gives students the opportunity to write and compose music in their English and language classes. Allow students to write prose , poetry, and lyrics instead of fiction. Encourage students to incorporate original music into their assignments, projects, or presentations.
4. Incorporate music into math. The research has shown that music can and will lead to better numeracy. Math and music are full of patterns and sequences. Use popular music to show students the existence of math in its creation.

5. Music is a series of words and ideas conveyed through sound. Reading and understanding the development of music can enhance the development of a critical mind. It can enable students to analyze and synthesize the meanings behind the music and the words.

6. Physical activity is enhanced by music. Go to any gym in the country and what do you hear, stimulating music that attacks the senses and motivates to keep on trying to be physically fit. Let the dancing and moving begin.

In 1998 a group of ten leading educational organizations in the United States, including the American Association of School Administrators, American Federation of Teachers, National Education Association, National Parent Teacher Association, and the National School Boards Association, adopted a Statement of Principles regarding "The Value and Quality of Arts Education." This statement outlines the following seven principles:

1. Every student in America should have an education in the arts.

2. To ensure a basic education in the arts for all students, the arts should be recognized as serious, core academic subjects.

3. Education policy makers should incorporate the multiple lessons of recent research concerning the value and impact of arts education.

4. A comprehensive sequential curriculum and qualified arts teachers must be recognized as the basis and core for substantive arts education by all students.

5. Arts education programs should be grounded in rigorous instruction, provide meaningful assessment of academic progress and performance, and take their place within a structure of direct accountability to school officials, parents, and the community.

6. Community resources that provide exposure to the arts, enrichment, and entertainment through the arts all offer valuable support and enhancement to an in-school arts education ... however, these kinds of activities cannot substitute for a comprehensive, balanced, sequential arts education taught by qualified teachers.

7. We support those programs, policies, and practitioners that reflect these principles.

These principles were created fifteen years ago and we are still struggling to achieve these in our American school system. How long must we continue the conversation toward change? When will all educators realize that the arts are one of the foundational stones of human existence and enjoyment? Hopefully soon!

3 TIPS FOR TEACHERS

1. Figure out ways to build the arts (including music) into your lessons.
2. Encourage your students to pursue music or other arts and explain how this will help their brains and minds develop.
3. Lobby for strong programs in the arts at your school and support the arts and artistic performances of your students.

REFERENCES

Art in Action (n.d). Why Art? Retrieved August 6, 2013, from http://www.artinaction.org/w/whyart .

Church. E. B. (2013). Learning Through the Arts. Retrieved August 6, 2013, from http://www.scholastic.com/teachers/article/learning-through-arts.

Gazzanga, M., Asbury, C., and Rich, B. (2008). Learning, Arts and the Brain. The Dana Consortium Reports on Arts and Cognition. Retrieved August 6, 2013, from http://www.dana.org/uploadedFiles/News_and_Publications/Special_Publications/Learning,%20Arts%20and%20the%20Brain_ArtsAndCognition_Compl.pdf.

Sousa, D. (2006). How the Arts Develop the Young Brain. The School Administrator, December 2006, Number 11, Volume 63.

Sylwester, R. (1998). Art for the Brain Sake. Educational Leadership, November 1998, Volume 56. Number 3.

Zattorre, R., and Salimpoor, V. (n.d.). Why Music Makes Our Brain Sing. NYTimes.com. *The New York Times—Breaking News, World News & Multimedia.* Retrieved October 9, 2013, from http://www.nytimes.com/2013/06/09/opinion/sunday/why-music-makes-our-brain-sing.html?_r=0.

Chapter Four

Language Development and Computing for Healthy Mind Development

Language is as fundamental to life as food. We as human beings need to be able to communicate to be able to survive. Language evolved as a way to communicate ideas, strategies, emotions, and a way to interact with one another socially and physically.

Children are not born with fully developed language abilities, although they have innate brain structures that are designed for creating and interpreting language—both written and spoken. However, these abilities to engage meaningfully with language need to be taught and fostered through effective modeling and interaction with role models. This engagement occurs naturally with parents or others who interact daily with the child. Each child eventually begins with the understanding that certain sounds are associated with certain items or actions.

Researchers have found that language development begins before a child is even born, as a fetus is able to identify the speech and sound patterns of the mother's voice. By the age of four months, infants are able to discriminate sounds and even read lips.

Researchers have actually found that infants are able to distinguish between speech sounds from all languages, not just the native language spoken in their homes. However, this ability disappears around the age of ten months and children begin to only recognize the speech sounds of their native language. By the time a child reaches age three, he or she will have a vocabulary of approximately 3,000 words (Cherry, 2013).

Children seem to follow a similar pattern of language development. Starting at the age of three to nine months the first stage is of pre-linguistic babbling which includes sounds like ooo and aaa and ma ma ba. At the age of ten–thirteen months they begin the holophase stage where they produce their first words. However, their comprehension of words is almost double what they are able to speak. At the age of eighteen months they are able to produce two word sentences and begin to differentiate between nouns and verbs. Finally at age two–three they express multi-word sentences and communicate in a way that they are understood by the people around them. As children age, they continue to learn more new words every day. By the time they enter school around the age of five, children typically have a vocabulary of 10,000 words or more.

If children are able to enter school with a vocabulary of 10,000 words or more, what happens once they are in school? Why are there children who have language delays? What happens during the early stages of language acquisition that does not register or result in effective communication?

Early development of number concepts is also critical in developing mathematical skills as well as positive attitudes about mathematics at an early age. Special methods and activities will assist children to develop early numeracy skills. These methods will need to include the use of motivating and engaging concrete materials that children can manipulate. Young children need to experience a lot of "doing" and "saying" before written numerals will make sense to them (Russell, 2013). How can we best prepare young children to develop numeracy and literacy to prepare them for a lifetime?

NATURE OF THE ISSUE AND HOW IT AFFECTS CHILDREN

According to David Sousa and other literacy experts, reading is the most challenging task we ask the young brain to do. Unlike spoken language, reading is not a task that the brain learns to do without support. We need to spend a great deal of time with each individual child to build solid literacy skills early and help develop them as solidly as possible with repeated practice and feedback on that practice. Children need to learn solidly the sounds that letters make, and then build on these. The brain of readers is changed once it learns to read. Good readers and poor readers process text differently in their brains.

Sally Shaywitz at Yale Medical school has shown that these differences in the brains of poor readers and good readers can be fixed by purposeful training and engagement with letter sounds. Stanislas Dehaene (2013) in his article "Inside the Letterbox: How Literacy Transforms the Human Brain" shows that "learning to read changes the *visual* brain. However, our study of literate and illiterate brains also uncovered a massive and positive effect of literacy on the network for *spoken* language processing."

He further argues that "learning to read is a major event in a child's life. Cognitive neuroscience shows why: compared to the brain of an illiterate person, the literate brain is massively changed, mostly for the better. . . . Once children learn to read, their brains are literally different." Children with reading difficulties show different patterns in the way they read according to Sally Shaywitz at Yale, but with purposeful training, many children can overcome these differences and their brains will operate more like good readers.

Children who enter school with delays or deficits in language or math development often fall behind very quickly within the classroom. Kindergarten and first grade are packed with skills that enhance language and analytical thinking that is required to do math and literacy. Children realize very quickly that they are behind and often disengage which masks as lack of motivation—and in some cases behavioral problems can develop to mask the learning difficulties. Children need to be literate and able to use math to be able to survive and be a productive member of society.

In the last five years Response to Intervention, a special education strategy, has been in the forefront of remediation for children who are experiencing learning, language, or mathematical deficits. The model focus is comprised of three tiers: Tier 1 which is initiated in the classroom with best practices, Tier 2 which involves targeted strategies within small group instruction, and Tier 3 which is intense individualized programming. If children are unsuccessful in the RTI model they are often referred to special education provided there is a documented disability. For many children their difficulties are usually identified as Learning Disabilities (Literacy and Mathematical functioning) and/or speech and language.

The key to remediation is early identification and programming. Educators are now better able to help children experiencing difficulties as the repertoire of skills and tools have been enhanced to assess and meet the needs of these young children earlier than was previously seen.

It is crucial that all children receive an excellent foundation in the two critical skills of literacy and numeracy, so as to be successful in life. The absence of these two skills will severely impact one's chances of having a fulfilling or happy life.

ONGOING STRATEGIES TO IMPROVE THE ISSUE

Language and Literacy

It is important that any type of language or literacy program include the following:

1. Students have a clear understanding of the expectations.

2. Instruction provided matches the individual's readiness and level.
3. Instruction is explicit and direct.
4. Students are grouped appropriately using documented evidence for level.
5. Instruction includes frequent opportunities for feedback and interaction.
6. Students are provided many opportunities to read on their own and with support as needed while fluency is developing.

Comprehension is a key skill in language and literacy acquisition. The following components are foundational in improving or developing comprehension:

- Activating background knowledge
- Predicting
- Generating and answering questions
- Clarifying
- Summarizing
- Using text structures
- Monitoring comprehension
- Engaging text and conversations about reading (Vaughn, Bos, Schum, 2011)

Techniques for Teaching Decoding and Sight Words

Techniques include:

- Making words, word sorting, and word walls
- DISSECT strategy

   1. Discover the word's content
   2. Isolate the prefix
   3. Separate the suffix
   4. Say the stem
   5. Examine the stem
   6. Check with someone
   7. Try the dictionary (Vaughn, Bos, Schum, 2011)

Strategies for Teaching Word Identification

Teaching sight words:

- Automaticity
- High-frequency words

Teaching decoding strategies:

- Phonic analysis
- Onset-rime
- Structural analysis
- Syllabication
- Syntax and semantics (Vaughn, Bos, Schum, 2011)

When teaching language skills to children it is imperative that you begin with strategies that are easily integrated and can produce results in a timely way. The following are a variety of strategies that develop phonological abilities and letter recognition:

- Teach a core set of frequently used consonants and short vowel sounds.
- Begin immediately to blend and segment the sounds.
- Separate the introduction of letter sounds with similar auditory and visual features.
- Use consistent key words to assist students in hearing and remembering the sound.
- Teach that some letters can represent more than one sound.
- Teach that different letters can make the same sound.
- Teach that sounds can be represented by a single letter or combination of letters.
- Color-code consonants and vowels.
- Add a kinesthetic component.
- Have students use mirrors and feel their mouths (Vaughn, Bos, Schum, 2011).

The number of available strategies for remediation of language and literacy is formidable, as there are hundreds of books written. This list is but a small sample of what can be done to help in this area.

Mathematical skills and numeracy also have ongoing strategies with demonstrated success. A comprehensive literature review published by the National Dissemination Center for Children with Disabilities called Effective Mathematics Instruction by Kathlyn Steedly, Kyrie Dragoo, Sousan Arefeh, and Stephen Luke found that four particular methods of teaching were most promising for improving mathematical skills:

- *Systematic and explicit instruction*, a detailed instructional approach in which teachers guide students through a defined instructional sequence. Within systematic and explicit instruction students learn to regularly apply strategies that effective learners use as a fundamental part of mastering concepts.

- *Self-instruction*, through which students learn to manage their own learning with specific prompting or solution-oriented questions.
- *Peer tutoring*, an approach that involves pairing students together to learn or practice an academic task.
- *Visual representation*, which uses manipulatives, pictures, number lines, and graphs of functions and relationships to teach mathematical concepts.

WHAT YOU CAN DO: TIPS FOR PARENTS

Mathematics and Language Development

The tips below highlight ways that you can help a child learn early math skills by building on their natural curiosity and having fun together. (Note: Most of these tips are designed for older children—ages two–three. Younger children can be exposed to stories and songs using repetition, rhymes, and numbers.) This list can be used by parents, adults or early years pre-school teachers.

- *Play with shape-sorters.* Talk with your child about each shape—count the sides, describe the colors. Make your own shapes by cutting large shapes out of colored construction paper. Ask your child to "hop on the circle" or "jump on the red shape."
- *Count and sort.* Gather together a basket of small toys, shells, pebbles, or buttons. Count them with your child. Sort them based on size, color, or what they do (i.e., all the cars in one pile, all the animals in another).
- *Place the call.* With your three year old, begin teaching her the address and phone number of your home. Talk with your child about how each house has a number, and how their house or apartment is one of a series, each with its own number.
- *What size is it?* Notice the sizes of objects in the world around you: That pink pocketbook is the biggest. The blue pocketbook is the smallest. Ask your child to think about his own size relative to other objects ("Do you fit under the table? Under the chair?").
- *You're cookin' now!* Even young children can help fill, stir, and pour. Through these activities, children learn, quite naturally, to count, measure, add, and estimate.
- *Walk it off.* Taking a walk gives children many opportunities to compare (which stone is bigger?), assess (how many acorns did we find?), note similarities and differences (does the duck have fur like the bunny does?) and categorize (see if you can find some red leaves). You can also talk about size (by taking big and little steps), estimate distance (is the park close to our house or far away?), and practice counting (let's count how many steps until we get to the corner).

- *Picture time.* Use an hourglass, stopwatch, or timer to time short (one–three minute) activities. This helps children develop a sense of time and to understand that some things take longer than others.
- *Shape up.* Point out the different shapes and colors you see during the day. On a walk, you may see a triangle-shaped sign that's yellow. Inside a store you may see a rectangle-shaped sign that's red.
- *Read and sing your numbers.* Sing songs that rhyme, repeat, or have numbers in them. Songs reinforce patterns (which is a math skill as well). They also are fun ways to practice language and foster social skills like cooperation.
- *Start today.* Use a calendar to talk about the date, the day of the week, and the weather. Calendars reinforce counting, sequences, and patterns. Build logical thinking skills by talking about cold weather and asking your child: What do we wear when it's cold? This encourages your child to make the link between cold weather and warm clothing.
- *Pass it around.* Ask for your child's help in distributing items like snacks or in laying napkins out on the dinner table. Help him give one cracker to each child. This helps children understand one-to-one correspondence. When you are distributing items, emphasize the number concept: "One for you, one for me, one for Daddy." Or, "We are putting on our shoes: One, two."
- *Big on blocks.* Give your child the chance to play with wooden blocks, plastic interlocking blocks, empty boxes, milk cartons, etc. Stacking and manipulating these toys helps children learn about shapes and the relationships between shapes (e.g., two triangles make a square). Nesting boxes and cups for younger children helps them understand the relationship between different sized objects.
- *Tunnel time.* Open a large cardboard box at each end to turn it into a tunnel. This helps children understand where their body is in space and in relation to other objects.
- *The long and the short of it.* Cut a few (three–five) pieces of ribbon, yarn, or paper in different lengths. Talk about ideas like long and short. With your child, put in order of longest to shortest.
- *Learn through touch.* Cut shapes—circle, square, triangle—out of sturdy cardboard. Let your child touch the shape with her eyes open and then closed.
- *Pattern play.* Have fun with patterns by letting children arrange dry macaroni, chunky beads, different types of dry cereal, or pieces of paper in different patterns or designs. Supervise your child carefully during this activity to prevent choking, and put away all items when you are done.
- *Laundry learning.* Make household jobs fun. As you sort the laundry, ask your child to make a pile of shirts and a pile of socks. Ask him which pile is the bigger (estimation). Together, count how many shirts. See if he can

make pairs of socks: Can you take two socks out and put them in their own pile? (Don't worry if they don't match! This activity is more about counting than matching.)

- *Playground math.* As your child plays, make comparisons based on height (high/low), position (over/under), or size (big/little).
- *Dress for math success.* Ask your child to pick out a shirt for the day. Ask: What color is your shirt? Yes, yellow. Can you find something in your room that is also yellow? As your child nears three and beyond, notice patterns in his clothing—like stripes, colors, shapes, or pictures: I see a pattern on your shirt. There are stripes that go red, blue, red, blue. Or, your shirt is covered with ponies—a big pony next to a little pony, all over your shirt!
- *Graphing games.* As your child nears three and beyond, make a chart where your child can put a sticker each time it rains or each time it is sunny. At the end of a week, you can estimate together which column has more or less stickers, and count how many to be sure (List from Zero to 3 National Center for Toddlers, Infants and Children).

Classification Activities:

1. Use blocks to engage young children to repeat the patterns—blue, green, orange, etc.
2. Ask young children to sort the silverware or the laundry based on color.
3. Use shapes to encourage children to determine what comes next—triangle, square, circle, triangle, etc.
4. Ask children to think of everything they can write with, ride on, that swims, that flies, etc.
5. Ask children how many items in the living room are square or round or heavy, etc.
6. Ask them to tell you how many things are made of wood, plastic, metal, etc.
7. Extend classification activities to include more than one attribute (heavy and small, or square and smooth, etc.)

More Pre-Number Activities:

1. Draw a number of circles (faces) and put down a number of buttons for eyes. Ask the child if there are enough eyes for the faces and how they can find out. Repeat this activity for mouths, noses, etc. Speak in terms of more than and less than or as many as and how can we find out.

2. Use stickers to make patterns on a page or classify them by attributes. Arrange a row of a set number of stickers, arrange a second row with more spaces between the stickers, and ask the child if there are the same number of stickers or more or less. Ask how they can find out— DON'T COUNT! Match the stickers one to one.

3. Arrange items on a tray (toothbrush, comb, spoon, etc.), ask the child to look away, and rearrange the items to see if they realize the number of items is still the same or if they think it's different.

Key Math Skills for School

More advanced mathematical skills are based on an early math "foundation"—just like a house is built on a strong foundation. In the toddler years, one can help a child begin to develop early math skills by introducing ideas like Number Sense: This is the ability to count accurately—first forward. Then, later in school, children will learn to count backward. A more complex skill related to number sense is the ability to see relationships between numbers—like adding and subtracting.

1. Representation: Making mathematical ideas "real" by using words, pictures, symbols, and objects (like blocks).

2. Spatial sense: Later in school, children will call this "geometry." But for toddlers it is introducing the ideas of shape, size, space, position, direction, and movement.

3. Measurement: Technically, this is finding the length, height, and weight of an object using units like inches, feet, or pounds. Measurement of time (in minutes, for example) also falls under this skill area.

4. Estimation: This is the ability to make a good guess about the amount or size of something. This is very difficult for young children to do. You can help them by showing them the meaning of words like more, less, bigger, smaller, more than, less than.

5. Patterns: Patterns are things—numbers, shapes, images—that repeat in a logical way. Patterns help children learn to make predictions, to understand what comes next, to make logical connections, and to use reasoning skills.

6. Problem-solving: The ability to think through a problem, to recognize there is more than one path to the answer. It means using past knowledge and logical thinking skills to find an answer (From Diezmann & Yelland, 2000, and Fromboluti & Rinck, 1999).

In conclusion, language and math skills are at the core of a successful life in the 21st century. Children who experience difficulties need to receive the necessary supports and instruction as soon as the problem has been identified. Early intervention is key to remediation. Every child deserves the chance to receive excellent teaching and an education that will help them prosper and be successful in any path they choose to pursue. It is the responsibility of the educational system and society to make sure that all children receive what they need to be literate and functional in mathematical ability.

REFERENCES

Cherry, K. (2013). All Stages of Early Development. Retrieved August 7, 2013, from http://psychology.about.com/od/developmentalpsychology/ss/early-childhood-development_3.htm.

Dehaene, S. (2013, June 3). The Dana Foundation. *Brain and Brain Research Information—Dana Foundation*. Retrieved October 9, 2013, from http://www.dana.org/news/cerebrum/detail.aspx?id=43644.

Diezmann, C., and Yelland, N. J. (2000). Developing mathematical literacy in the early childhood years. In Yelland, N. J. (Ed.), Promoting meaningful learning: Innovations in educating early childhood professionals (pp.47–58). Washington, DC: National Association for the Education of Young Children.

Fromboluti, C. S., and Rinck, N. (1999, June). Early childhood: Where learning begins. U.S. Department of Education, Office of Educational Research and Improvement, National Institute on Early Childhood Development and Education. Retrieved September 22, 2012, from http://www.kidsource.com/education/math/whatis.html.

Russell, D. (2013). Pre-School Math. Retrieved August 7, 2013, from http://math.about.com/od/reference/a/preschool.htm.

Steedly, K., Dragoo, K., Arefeh, S., and Luke, S. (n.d.). Effective Mathematics Instruction. *National Dissemination Center for Children with Disabilities*. Retrieved November 4, 2013, from http://nichcy.org/research/ee/math.

National Center for Infants, Toddlers and Children Zero to 3 (n.d.) Early Math Skills. Retrieved August 7, 2013, from http://www.zerotothree.org/child-development/early-development/supporting-early-math-skills.html.

Vaughn, S., Bos, & Schumm (2011). Teaching Students Who Are Exceptional and at Risk, 5th Ed. Person Education Inc. NYC.

Part II

Challenges to Brain and Mind Health

Chapter Five

Attention: The Problem of Focus!

The children growing up in the media generation believe they can multitask effectively. They truly believe that they can listen to music, play video games while reading, talk on the phone, and do homework while watching television. Perhaps this is extreme, but the truth is, the brain cannot do two complex cognitive tasks at once. It can switch in such a way that it may seem like it can, but alas, it cannot. And in the time that it takes to switch attention from one cognitive task (fractions of a second) to another, accidents happen and problems occur and learning is disrupted.

As John Medina (2012), author of "Brain Rules" wrote,

> multitasking, when it comes to paying attention, is a myth. The brain naturally focuses on concepts sequentially, one at a time. At first that might sound confusing; at one level the brain does multitask. You can walk and talk at the same time. Your brain controls your heartbeat while you read a book. Pianists can play a piece with the left hand and right hand simultaneously. Surely this is multitasking. But I am talking about the brain's ability to pay attention. It is the resource you forcibly deploy while trying to listen to a boring lecture at school. It is the activity that collapses as your brain wanders during a tedious presentation at work. This attentional ability is not capable of multitasking.

Why is the myth of multitasking so problematic for children (and adults)? What are some of the learning issues associated with the myth of multitasking?

NATURE OF THE PROBLEM

Texting and even talking on the phone especially for the novice driver is so dangerous. The brain simply cannot refocus attention that quickly and completely, and for those "expert drivers" problems happen in a fraction of a second. And because the novice driver's brain is not organized like the more "expert" driver (whose brain has automated many aspects of driving so these are not conscious), the novice driver must think through nearly every aspect of what he or she is doing consciously. Medina (2012) wrote:

> A good example [of dangerous multi-tasking] is driving while talking on a cell phone. Until researchers started measuring the effects of cell-phone distractions under controlled conditions, nobody had any idea how profoundly they can impair a driver. It's like driving drunk. Recall that large fractions of a second are consumed every time the brain switches tasks. Cell-phone talkers are a half-second slower to hit the brakes in emergencies, slower to return to normal speed after an emergency, and more wild in their "following distance" behind the vehicle in front of them. In a half-second, a driver going 70 mph travels 51 feet. Given that 80 percent of crashes happen within three seconds of some kind of driver distraction, increasing your amount of task-switching increases your risk of an accident. More than 50 percent of the visual cues spotted by attentive drivers are missed by cell-phone talkers. Not surprisingly, they get in more wrecks than anyone except very drunk drivers.

The same is true for school and schoolwork—although not as immediately life threatening. Children and adolescents (and adults for that matter) who are learning new ideas, skills, concepts, and content must think carefully and consciously about these—that is, they must devote a great deal of cognitive effort to these. Any interference is problematic and disrupts attention in the process.

Turn off the competition. We've had many students say "but I MUST have the television on when I study . . . or music . . . it's just background noise." Here's the problem with this statement. If you need background noise get a sound machine or play white noise or turn on a fan. You can also play music that does not have words—or music that you do not know well.

However, once you know the music or have television with dialog (and as we will learn in chapter 12, television has qualities inherent in its makeup that makes it nearly impossible to disengage attention from it), your brain will flip flop back and forth between the different verbal information—that which you are supposed to be "reading" and the words of the song or dialog on the television or the texts coming through or the e-mails. The brain will retain virtually nothing from the task that is cognitively more demanding (reading, writing, mathematics, problem solving, or other school work) when multitasking with something that is less cognitively demanding (listening to music, watching television, texting, talking on the phone).

For effective and efficient work, the brain needs to eliminate opportunities for distraction. Can the brain handle any distraction? How much is too much? What about those with attention problems? How can we improve our attention? At what point are attention problems truly problems?

BRAIN FUNCTION: SELECTIVE ATTENTION

To interact effectively with the people around you, your brain must constantly process large amounts of more or less complex information. However, it can only carry out a limited number of tasks at a time, so it needs to select the most relevant information, based on your needs at any given moment (Brain Center America, 2013). Certain functions governed by the brain are fairly automatic and unconscious—for example, vital functions like breathing or highly developed skills such as competitive running. As a result, you don't have to specifically focus on the level of oxygen in your blood in order to activate your diaphragm and fill your lungs.

Other functions require constant supervision. When you are reading a text or sign it means a more or less conscious and sustained mental effort and attention. Your attention span varies depending on the type of information you're looking for, and it relies on the proper function of much of your brain. Exercising your attention span by performing a variety of specifically designed exercises promotes the proper functioning of many areas of the brain (Brain Center America, 2013).

Your prefrontal cortex, located at the front of your brain, governs attention span and provides additional supervision; in other words, it determines what information is to be given priority and which cognitive resources are needed to analyze this information and eliminate any distractions. It does a wonderful automatic job of sorting and categorizing for you as to where you will need to focus your attention. Human beings are not natural multi-taskers; the brain functions at optimal level when it only does one thing at a time.

Male and female alike, if you ask it to do two somewhat complicated tasks at the same time, your performance levels for each will be reduced by half. People whom we admire for their multitasking ability are actually high-performance individuals who can quickly and efficiently complete each of the tasks one after the other (Brain Center America, 2013). Generally they have very efficient and high-speed brains. Often they are experts in one of the areas in which they are multitasking.

The ability to focus on some things at the expense of others is crucial for functioning in a complicated world. But studies show there can be a downside to this focus—too much attention to one thing may make us seemingly "blind" or "deaf" to other stimuli in the environment. We are curious and want to try to understand and hear everything that is happening at once. The brain tries very hard to take in what it can. Our brains recreate an internal map of the world we see through our eyes, mapping our visual field onto specific brain cells.

Humans and our primate relatives have the ability to pay attention to objects in the visual scene without looking at them directly (Farran et al., 2013). "Essentially, we 'see out of the corner of our eyes,' as the old saying goes. This ability helps us detect threats, and react quickly to avoid them, as when a car running a red light at high speed is approaching from our side (Mangun, 2013). Even though we can see from the corner of our eye we are not able to attend to all of the stimuli that are present within our personal bubble space, which is about 3–5 feet around us.

The problem of consciousness continues to be a subject of great debate in cognitive science. Synthesizing decades of research, *The Conscious Brain,* written by Jesse Prinz (2012), advances a new theory of the psychological and neurophysiological correlates of conscious experience. Prinz's account of consciousness makes two main claims: first consciousness always arises at a particular stage of perceptual processing—the intermediate level, and, second, consciousness depends on attention. Attention changes the flow of information allowing perceptual information to access memory systems. Neurobiologically this change in flow depends on synchronized neural firing. Neural synchrony is also implicated in the unity of consciousness and in the temporal duration of experience.

Prinz also explores the limits of consciousness. We have no direct experience of our thoughts, no experience of motor commands, and no experience of a conscious self. All consciousness is perceptual, and it functions to make perceptual information available to systems that allow for flexible behavior.

DO TELEVISION AND VIDEO GAMES AFFECT ATTENTION?

Some experts have argued that watching too many fast-paced television programs and video games may actually increase the likelihood of attention problems. If the brain becomes accustomed to constant stimulation by rapidly changing visual effects, it may easily become impatient with tasks that require closer attention. Television also makes fewer demands on attention than do reading, studying, or playing a game.

Without enough of these more challenging activities, the brain may "get out of shape" (Human Diseases and Conditions, 2013). The brain will typically choose the path of least resistance or cognitive strain, and if given a steady diet of tasks that require little to no cognitive strain, it will be difficult to make the brain work hard on a more cognitively challenging task.

However, the reverse may be true. Children and adults with limited attention resources may be attracted to intense stimulation and therefore may be captured by television or video games. Less intense activities may not hold the focus of individuals with attention deficits. More research is needed to better understand this issue.

We don't pay attention to boring things. What we pay attention to is profoundly influenced by memory. Our previous experience predicts where we should pay attention. Culture matters too. Whether in school or in business, these differences can greatly affect how an audience perceives a given presentation.

We pay attention to things like emotions, threats, and sex. Regardless of who you are, the brain pays a great deal of attention to these questions: Can I eat it? Will it eat me? Can I mate with it? Will it mate with me? Have I seen it before? The brain is not capable of multitasking. We can talk and breathe, but when it comes to higher level tasks, we just can't do it.

Driving while talking on a cell phone is like driving drunk. The brain is a sequential processor and large fractions of a second are consumed every time the brain switches tasks. This is why cell-phone talkers are a half-second slower to hit the brakes and get in more wrecks (Medina, 2012).

Workplaces and schools actually encourage this type of multitasking. Walk into any office and you'll see people sending e-mails, answering their phones, Instant Messaging, and on MySpace—all at the same time. Research shows your error rate goes up 50 percent and it takes you twice as long to do things (Medina, 2012). When you're always online you're always distracted. So the always online organization is the always unproductive organization.

ONGOING STRATEGIES

There are a variety of strategies that can be used with students, employees, and family members when it comes to attention and focus. Below you will find some suggestions. The list is not exhaustive and it is recommended that the correct strategy be chosen for the right individual.

There are nine types of adaptations for anyone who is experiencing attention problems. These adaptations can work in a school or professional work environment.

1. Size: Adapt the number of items that the learner/worker is expected to learn or complete.
2. Input: Adapt the way the instruction or training is delivered to the learner.
3. Participation: Adapt the extent to which the learner/worker is actively involved in the task.
4. Time: Adapt the time allotted and allowed for learning, task completion, and/or testing.

5. Difficulty: Adapt the skill level, problem type, or the rules on how the learner/worker may approach the work.
6. Alternate Goals: Adapt the goals or outcome expectations while using the same materials.
7. Level of Support: Increase the amount of personal assistance with a specific learner/worker.
8. Output: Adapt how the learner/worker can respond to instruction or training.
9. Substitute Curriculum-Content: Provide different instruction and materials to meet a learner/worker's individual goals (Indiana University, 2010).

There are a variety of general accommodations for students with attention/behavior problems. It is important to remember that not all of these accommodations or strategies will work for all students. The individual needs of each student need to be taken into consideration before the application of these strategies. This is but a short list of possibilities.

Literacy:

1. Second set of books at home
2. Books on tape
3. Interactive CD reading programs
4. Hand-held spell checker

Writing:

1. Computers
2. Graph paper
3. Dictate responses
4. Pencil or pen with rubber grip
5. Form-filling software
6. Keyguards
7. Color-coded notebooks
8. Give photocopied notes
9. Have student use highlighter
10. Outline of key points of presentation or lesson

Groups:

1. Work in cooperative mixed-ability groups
2. Peer assistance pairings

3. Clear rules and expectations for group behavior
4. Assign job or specific responsibility
5. Headphones for privacy
6. Taped instructions
7. Buddy system
8. Five-minute warning for transitions

Presentations/Discussions/Questioning:

1. Alternative methods of presentation (visual, videotape, graphs, maps, pictures)
2. Provide visual aids
3. Provide model of previous work or examples
4. Detail descriptions or checklist of project components
5. Place student near or in front of teacher or audience
6. Provide stimuli-reduced environments
7. Repeat question before answering
8. Provide time to process before answering questions

When making accommodations for a child with attention issues it is imperative that the strategy matches the age level and learning level of the student. Being aware of these simple factors can accelerate behavior problems and power struggles. As a teacher one must use a variety of visual and auditory teaching techniques to stimulate interest and maintain focus. Teachers and parents must use close proximity control to assist the student in focusing on the directions and understanding the task that is being asked of them. If the adult wants to modify the child's behavior one needs to catch the student being good and/or doing the right thing. Giving immediate praise or rewards will often shape behavior in a way that allows the child to meet the expectations.

Sometimes children and young adults have attention challenges that go beyond those that are based on the environment. Improving one's mindfulness (which will be discussed at length in the section on strategies) will also improve control over one's brain and attention. However, sometimes children have attention disorders that are not helped by basic interventions such as increasing mindfulness and meditation. Attention disorders fall into three types: Attention Deficit Disorder, Attention Deficit Hyperactivity Disorder, and Not Otherwise Specified Attention Disorder. Students can exhibit Predominantly Inattentive Type, Predominantly Hyperactivity/Impulsive Type, and the combined type.

Effects of the disorder within the classroom can be seen in behavioral problems, becoming frustrated and aggressive, and experiencing failure on tests and assignments. A very large impact of having an attention challenge is

that it impairs social relations whereas the student struggles with social interactions because of the lack of social skills. These students are often disorganized and lose their materials frequently.

The effects of this disorder at home can be manifested by children not
listening to their parents and waging battles over the smallest detail. Both
parties become argumentative over daily chores, roles, and responsibilities.
Oftentimes there is frustration for both adult and child because the child is
unable to complete even the simple tasks without supervision or support.
Teachers and parents alike should be on the look-out for pervasive patterns
of attention problems that cannot seem to be managed well by typical levels
of support.

THREE TIPS FOR TEACHERS

1. Remember that students don't pay attention to boring things—keep
   students engaged with interesting lessons and help them see the rele-
   vance of what they are learning and make connections as much as
   possible.
2. Encourage parents to set limits on children's interactions with television and other video games/screens and spend more time on cognitive
   tasks that are challenging without these distractions.
3. Make sure that drivers of all ages realize how dangerous it is to text,
   talk on the phone, or engage in other cognitive tasks competing for
   attention, and encourage them to avoid distracted driving.

RESOURCES

- Neuroscience for Kids is an extensive and entertaining website maintained
  by Research Associate Professor Eric Chudler at the University of Washington, Seattle. It features easy-to-understand information on a range of
  topics related to the brain and nervous system, including attention. http://
  faculty.washington.edu/chudler/neurok.html.
- KidsHealth.org from the Nemours Foundation posts information about
  attention deficit disorders and other issues concerning learning
  (www.KidsHealth.org). Read more at http://www.humanillnesses.com/
  Behavioral-Health-A-Br/Attention.html#ixzz2cA1miSyVBooks.
- Powledge, Tabitha M. *Your Brain: How You Got It and How It Works.*
  New York: Charles Scribner's Sons, 1994.
- Novitt-Moreno, Anne. *How Your Brain Works.* Emeryville, CA: ZiffDavis
  Press, 1995.

ORGANIZATIONS

- The website Neuroscience for Kids is a great resource for kids and teens about brain chemistry, structure, and function. It provides other resources and links as well. http://faculty.washington.edu/chudler/neurok.html.
- Nemours Center for Children's Health Media, Alfred I. duPont Hospital for Children, 1600 Rockland Road, Wilmington, DE 19803. This organization is dedicated to issues of children's health and produces the KidsHealth website. Its website has articles about the brain, emotions, and behavior. http://www.KidsHealth.org.
- Read more: http://www.humanillnesses.com/Behavioral-Health-A-Br/ Brain-Chemistry-Neurochemistry.html#ixzz2cA2JSKtN.

REFERENCES

Brain Center America (2013). Selective Attention, retrieved August 15, 2013, from http:// www.braincenteramerica.com/selectatt.php.
Briggs, F., Mangun, G. R., Usrey, W. M. (2013). Attention enhances synaptic efficacy and the signal-to-noise ratio in neural circuits. Nature, 2013; DOI: 10.1038/nature12276.
Human Diseases and Conditions (2013). Attention. Retrieved August 16, 2013 from http:// www.humanillnesses.com/Behavioral-Health-A-Br/Attention.html.
Indiana University (2010). Nine Types of Adaptations. Center for School and Community Integration, Institute for the study of Developmental Disabilities.
Medina, J. (2012). Brain Rules. Pear Press.
Prinz, J. J. (2012). The Conscious Brain: How Attention Engenders Experience. Oxford University Press.

Chapter Six

Brain Injuries and Brain Damage

As parents and teachers we must do what we can to protect the young developing brains and minds of children. This book has discussed many such ways. How can we prevent brain injuries? What happens if the brain is injured or damaged? What are some of the common causes of brain injury or damage among young people? What can be done?

Millions of schoolchildren participate in organized athletics. There are risks associated with participation, and some are more obvious than others. There are some hidden risks of which every parent and educator should be aware. This chapter discusses some of the common and increasing injuries associated with athletics that interfere with learning: concussions and traumatic brain injury, as well as bullying and hazing on athletic teams, are discussed.

NATURE OF THE ISSUE AND HOW IT AFFECTS CHILDREN

Athletics

An estimated 300,000 sports- and recreation-related head injuries of mild to moderate severity occur in the United States each year. Most can be classified as concussions (Centers for Disease Control at www.cdc.gov.). There was an inverse relationship between the number of soccer ball impacts to the head and verbal learning (David Janda, Cynthia Bir, and Angela Cheney).

A concussion, or mild traumatic brain injury (MTBI), is an injury to the brain and as such should always be taken seriously. Recognition of concussions when they first happen is critical to the prevention of additional brain injury or death. Children can experience concussions in any sport—including noncontact sports—by experiencing a blow to the head. Concussions among young participants are most common in the following sports: cycling, soccer, football, lacrosse, field hockey, ice hockey, baseball, softball, basketball, skiing, and horseback riding. However, those sports in which there is a greater likelihood for collisions—especially at high speeds—have higher risk. In addition, activities like heading a soccer ball at young ages, while the brain is developing, can be problematic for brain development.

> "I actually just got a concussion a couple weeks ago. I was riding my snowmobile and lost control going around a corner at about sixty mph. I landed on the back of my head and fortunately was wearing a helmet. I had a pounding headache and felt nauseous for about 24 hours, but I never went to the hospital"(College junior).

Many concussions, like the one in the above example, go unreported, or medical attention is not sought because sometimes the symptoms are somewhat mild, like headache and dizziness. Once one has had a head injury like a concussion, he or she is at higher risk for another one. There are a couple of important hidden or lesser-known dangers associated with head injuries like concussions.

Perhaps the most serious is that if one suffers another concussion before fully recovering from the first (typically within a short period of time), this experience, called second-impact syndrome, can lead to brain swelling, possibly even permanent brain damage or death. (Institute of Medicine, 2002 and CDC.gov).

> "I had two concussions [sic] from snowboarding during high school, and had to wear a neck brace after the bus accident. I was also diagnosed with transverse myleitis [sic] during the beginning of my 8th grade year. At first they thought I had a brain tumor, and thought I would need to have a nasty operation. I was picked on at school by some of my friends when I came back from the hospital. They were trying to make light of the situation but it really just hurt my feelings. As a result of that I have lost a lot of feeling in my right arm, and can't tell temperature differences in some fingers, and get bad migraines. But I am very lucky that's the only result" (College sophomore).

Many adults have become somewhat cavalier about concussions, but we need to take them all seriously and be even more vigilant if a young person receives a second concussion shortly after the first. Some very helpful guides and fact sheets have been developed for coaches, parents, teachers, and all interested adults.

For example, the CDC developed the following fact sheet for parents and coaches that included the following "signs and symptoms" of a concussion, indicating that any one or more of these symptoms may indicate a concussion and to seek medical attention immediately if you suspect a child might have one. Signs observed if a child has a concussion:

- Appears dazed or stunned
- Is confused
- Forgetful
- Unsure of parts of game (score, opponent)
- Clumsy
- Slow in talking and movement
- Loss of consciousness
- Behavior/personality change
- Unable to recall events before or after injury

Athlete symptoms reported include:

- Headache
- Nausea
- Dizzy/balance problems
- Double or fuzzy vision
- Sluggish, foggy, groggy
- Sensitive to light
- Memory problems/confusion (CDC's tools for coaches www.cdc.gov, p. 4)

Medical attention should be sought immediately if you suspect a young person has a concussion. Even more important, the youngster should stop immediately whatever activity caused the head injury in the first place to avoid second-impact syndrome.

Hidden Dangers

Heading the soccer ball. A recent research study, "An Evaluation of the Cumulative Concussive Effect of Soccer Heading in the Youth Population," by David Janda, Cynthia Bir, and Angela Cheney (International Journal of Injury Control and Safety Promotion 9, no. 1, [March 2002]), examined the impact of heading the soccer ball on learning. They looked at fifty-seven young soccer players (average age 11.5) and found that there was an "inverse relationship between the number of ball impacts and verbal learning" (2002, 25) with many (nearly half) of the participants complaining of headaches following heading.

"Concussions have occurred more than once in my lifetime. The soccer field was always the scene, and the goal post was usually the culprit" (College junior).

Young children, even adolescents (and adults for that matter), should be discouraged from heading soccer balls, particularly as young brains are still developing (up to age twenty-five). Damage can be done to the brain later in

life too. Clearly, in addition to heading soccer balls, dangers include collisions with other players and/or goalposts.

> "I received a concussion when I was snowboarding. I was going down the
> mountain and took a huge fall. I laid there for a second and started crying but
> got back up and snowboarded down the remainder of the mountain. I felt okay
> for about a half hour with only suffering a head ache. After the half hour I was
> completely delirious. I was with my brother who took me to a store, and he
> described to me how I was walking into clothing racks and completely out
> there, all of which I do not even remember" (College sophomore).

Kids are often asked to shake it off or keep going after a brain injury, often
because well-intentioned adults underestimate the possible risk to a child's
brain. We, as adults, must intervene to keep kids safe—and we need to be
especially protective of children's developing brains.

Traumatic Brain Injury in Athletics

From a parent's and educator's perspective, we should be very concerned
about any blow to the head as the long-term impact on a child's learning may
not be immediately apparent but may manifest itself in ways we might not
realize until adulthood, if ever. We must attend to these blows and do whatever possible to avoid them altogether.

Another significant problem resulting from a major blow to the head is
traumatic brain injury (TBI). The Centers for Disease Control follow the
prevalence of, and provide assistance and information about, TBI for caregivers. They define TBI as follows: "A traumatic brain injury (TBI) is caused
by a blow or jolt to the head or a penetrating head injury that disrupts the
normal function of the brain. Not all blows or jolts to the head result in a TBI.
The severity of a TBI may range from 'mild,' i.e., a brief change in mental
status or consciousness, to 'severe,' i.e., an extended period of unconscious-
ness or amnesia after the injury."

The CDC reports that of the 1.4 million people who experience a traumatic brain injury, 1.1 million are treated and released from emergency rooms,
235,000 are hospitalized, and 50,000 die. For children aged zero to fourteen,
of the reported cases of TBI, the CDC reports the following statistics:
435,000 annual emergency room visits, 37,000 hospitalizations, and 2,685
deaths. Of course, these are only the reported brain injuries. Many health
professionals believe that the number of TBIs is much higher as many brain
injuries go unreported.

According to the CDC's surveillance system, the number one cause of
TBI is falls (28 percent of reported cases). Car accidents comprise 20 percent, followed by being struck by or against something (19 percent) and
assaults (11 percent). Traumatic brain injury can be insidious—many young

people may be affected but unaware. It may affect learning in subtle ways and is perhaps responsible for some types of learning disabilities and difficulties. It is estimated that as many as one in fifty Americans has a TBI to the point that it impacts learning and ability to engage in basic functioning (e.g., long-term and short-term memory and retention of new ideas).

The CDC reports that TBI can cause a wide range of functional changes affecting thinking, sensation, language, and/or emotions. It can also cause epilepsy and increase the risk for conditions such as Alzheimer's disease, Parkinson's disease, and other brain disorders that become more prevalent with age (www.cdc.gov/ ncipc/tbi/TBI.htm, para. 12).

Bullying and Hazing on Sports Teams

> "My school had a huge hazing issue w/ the football team. One individual decided to speak out to prevent it in the future. He explained how he was held down while the senior football players stuck a banana up his rear end. He was also flipped around and "tea-bagged." The acting out players were only suspended one day and only had to sit out one game. The school decided to keep it within the school system, so not a lot was heard of it after that. Besides the school couldn't ensure his safety anymore, so he was forced to drop out of the school system" (College junior).

While bullying is addressed elsewhere in this book, there is concern about bullying on athletic teams in middle and high school. Also problematic, particularly on athletic teams, is hazing. Hazing includes initiation rituals or rites of passage or activities that group members are expected to engage in that humiliate or harm them emotionally or physically. Hazing happens to people at every developmental level who want to join a particular organization or group—and sometimes it can be subtle or very overt.

Most people believe hazing is just a part of adolescence, but it can be very harmful to one's psychological and/or physical health. Hazing is not just associated with fraternities and sororities but with athletics and other social groups, even in middle school. A government website for girls' health (www.girlshealth.gov) lists the following as common types of hazing:

- depriving rookies/new members of sleep and placing restrictions on their personal hygiene
- yelling at, swearing at, and insulting new members/rookies
- forcing them to wear embarrassing or humiliating clothing in public
- forcing them to eat vile substances or smear such on their skin
- branding them
- subjecting them to physical beatings
- demanding that they engage in binge drinking and play drinking games
- forcing sexual simulation and assaulting them sexually

No degree of hazing should be tolerated. Adults should intervene even in what may appear on the surface to be relatively "benign" hazing, such as in the following example:

> "All of the sports teams at my high school involved some sort of hazing. It was just something you went through. I played soccer, and I think many of the traditions were lost, but I do remember hearing my freshman year that they were going to make us jump into a manmade lake right on our school property that wasn't even fit for fish, bugs or birds let alone humans. That of course never happened to us, but freshman were mandated to carry all the soccer balls out to the field each day and the heavy jugs of water. We all did it so we all reinforced it on the younger grades once we were upper classman. Many jokes were made at the freshman's expense and nobody felt bad for them when they complained because of course we all felt that it was just a rite of passage" (College sophomore).

Accidents and Brain Damage

Accidents are the leading cause of injury death of children aged one to twenty-four. The number one killer is motor vehicle accidents, followed by (depending on the age group) drowning and fire accidents. Some accidents are preventable, and certainly steps can be taken to keep children safe from these all-too-common accidents. This chapter explores the most dangerous and common accidents, those involving motor vehicles, bicycles, fire, and water, and discusses strategies to reduce the risk of serious harm or death for children.

Motor Vehicle Accidents

Inexperienced or immature drivers are responsible for 40 percent of teen deaths from motor vehicle accidents. In addition, the failure to wear seat belts consistently and drinking alcohol and using other drugs make driving even more dangerous. Car seats and seat belts can help a great deal in reducing motor vehicle fatalities. For example, Osberg and DiScala (1992) showed that for children who died in car crashes, there was a significant difference between those who were restrained (2.4 percent) and those who were unrestrained (4.5 percent).

The good news is that seat belt use is on the rise. Although there have been reports from the National Safety Council that even though more than 75,000 lives were saved between 2004 and 2008 because of seat belt use, *young drivers* are among the *lowest users* of seat belts with blacks and males being among the subgroups who use seat belts less than other groups (National Safety Council).

More recently, the Children's Hospital of Philadelphia released a paper demonstrating that just restraining children is insufficient. Even though evidence has shown that children dying in car accidents has declined dramatically in the past twenty years, authorities propose that we must focus on making sure restraint devices fit properly and are correctly used.

Physicians interviewed in the Children's Hospital of Philadelphia piece suggest the following: For instance, infants should ride in a rear-facing child safety seat until they reach one year and twenty pounds. Children aged one to four, between twenty and forty pounds, should ride in a forward-facing car seat, not in a seat belt. "Premature graduation to safety belts raises the risk of 'seat belt syndrome,' injuries to the abdomen and spinal cord from an improperly positioned seat belt," said Dr. Durbin. Children over four years and forty pounds should use a booster seat until about age eight, when they can properly use a seat belt without a booster seat. And for all children twelve years old and younger, "the safest place is in a vehicle's rear seat," added Dr. Winston (1999, para. 4).

The Journal of the American Medical Association (JAMA) (2006) showed that children in child safety seats (car seats or booster seats) were safer than those children wearing seat belts alone. Researchers at the University of Michigan found, overall, approximately one in 1,000 children in a two-way crash died, with less than half (45 percent) of all children in restraint seats. One of six children (15.7 percent) were in the front seat, two thirds (67.6 percent) were in passenger cars, one of six (15.6 percent) were in pre-1990 model year vehicles, and 4 percent of cars were driven by teenage drivers.

Compared with seat belts alone, child safety seats were associated with a 21 percent reduction in risk of death. When excluding cases of serious misuse of safety seats or belts, the reduced risk of death was 28 percent. Also, even though many children resist sitting in the middle of the back seat, researchers have found this space to be the safest for properly restrained children (University of Buffalo, 2006). Consider the following scary "close calls" of a couple of college students:

> When I was little I was in a car accident in my dad's truck. I remember I was still in my car seat and we were only a minute from home. Some girl who had just gotten her license pulled out and hit the side of the car that I was on. Luckily no one was injured, but I know I was scared (College sophomore).
>
> I was in a car accident driving home one night from work. It was foggy and I lived on a country road. I was approaching a blind curve; I knew a car was approaching from the other direction because I could see headlights (even though I couldn't see the car). As I rounded the curve, the other car was completely in my lane, about 100 feet in front of me. We were both traveling 40–45 mph, so a collision was unavoidable. I was able to pull off the road prior to the collision so that the impact on my car was on the driver's side instead of head-on. I was cut in the head and face from some shattered glass and had a couple of bruises but was otherwise unhurt. I found out later that the other

driver had been drinking but not enough to be considered legally drunk (Twenty-year-old college sophomore).

Countless adolescents have high school experiences of loss like these:

"Between 9th and 10th grade, four of my classmates were out driving in the summertime and were speeding. There were 2 15-year-olds and 2 16-year-olds. Two of the boys were fraternal twins. They were going too fast around a corner and lost control of the car. One of the twins was ejected from the car and died due to internal trauma. The driver had to be taken out of the car by the "jaws of life" and the other two boys were hurt rather badly as well. The fraternal twin who passed away was in a coma for about 2 days before he died. This was the saddest funeral I ever went to. During my graduation, there was a memorial about him and we had to relive that tragic day all over again" (Twenty-year-old college sophomore).

Inexperience and driving while impaired contribute to the majority of fatal car crashes. As one of the examples above illustrates, having them in appropriate car seats reduces the risk for young children. But these children and adolescents can be harmed because of the inexperienced drivers on the road. Of our small sample of college-aged survey respondents, several had been in a car accident, and most of them were driving and still inexperienced.

A recent study commissioned by the Robert Wood Johnson Foundation (RWJF) found that "graduated teen driver's-licensing programs" were found to reduce deaths from car accidents. Graduate driver's-licensing programs include

- A learner's phase requiring a licensed driver to be in the vehicle for a young driver's first months of driving.
- An intermediate phase allowing new young drivers to drive only during daylight and early evening hours and/or with a limited number of passengers.
- Full licensure available after the intermediate phase and sometimes only at age 17 or older (RWJF, 2006).

These researchers credit the reduction in traffic deaths among young people also partly to the raising of the legal drinking age, mandating seat belt use, and stricter drunk-driving laws. In addition to auto accidents, there are also concerns about children being backed over by vehicles (approximately twenty-five hundred children are treated for back-over injuries according to the CDC, 2005), hit by cars (research has shown that kids are at higher risk of being run over or hit by larger cars such as SUVs, kidsandcars.org, 2007), and harmed or killed by heatstroke from being left in vehicles (this number has been steadily rising, kidsandcars.org).

Bicycle Accidents

Many young people have accidents on or falls from bicycles. According to a study in 2010 "children ages 5–14 years have the highest rate of bicycle-related injuries in the country. Bicycle helmets can prevent head and brain injuries, which represent the most serious type of bicycle-related injury . . . while there has been substantial progress in the number of children who always wear their helmets, more than half do not" (Dellinger & Kresnow, 2010). Clearly there is still work to be done to get every child riding a bicycle to wear a helmet and practice good bicycle safety.

The website for KidsHealth (www.kidshealth.org) reports that close to three hundred thousand children end up in the emergency room because of injuries from bike falls. And according to the Centers for Disease Control and Prevention, bike injuries made up 59 percent of emergency room visits for children aged fifteen and younger. Death from falls typically results from head injury (see chapter on brain injuries). The concern about head injury has resulted in states adopting helmet laws.

Laws mandating proper helmet wearing for youths riding bikes have helped to reduce the number of head injuries from bike crashes (although the evidence is inconsistent). For example, the bicycle and helmet statistics reported by the Bicycle Helmet Safety Institute (2008) found, "Helmet use in the U.S. varies by orders of magnitude in different areas and different sectors of our society. White collar commuters probably reach 80 percent, while inner city kids and rural kids would be 10 percent or less. Overall, our best wild guess is probably no more than 25 per cent."

Although the evidence is mixed on the impact of mandatory helmet laws on reducing fatalities, most generally studies report that for children aged four to twenty, there has been a reduction (National Highway Transportation Association, 2013). Still, of the 2011 deaths reported for cyclists, 69 percent of deaths were children aged fourteen or younger (National Highway Transportation Association, 2013). As adults, we must be consistent in enforcing the wearing of helmets, not only for younger children but for older adolescents as well.

Fire Injury and Death

According to the Centers for Disease Control and Prevention's statistics, the third leading cause of injury death for one- to four-year-olds is "unintentional fireburn," and this is the second leading cause of injury death for children aged five to nine.

I was 8 years old when my house burnt to the ground. I was staying over at my friend's house and my brother was supposed to stay at his friend's house. My mother had just served my father divorce papers and he was really upset. The only two people that were supposed to be in the house were my mom and dad. Years later, I found out that my father was trying to kill my mother the night our house burnt down. One fire was electrical and the other fire, my father started by flicking his cigarette on the living room carpet. It was devastating and we lost just about everything. If I was home that night, I would not be answering these questions on this survey because the electrical fire started in the room next to my bedroom (twenty-nine-year-old female).

This violent form of arson—with intent to harm or kill another—is rarer than the accidental or unintentional fires that start, but this example speaks to how devastating and deadly fires can be. The U.S. Fire Association (USFA) provided the following statistics about accidental fires for 2006:

- There were 3,245 civilians that lost their lives as the result of fire.
- There were 16,400 civilian injuries that occurred as the result of fire.
- There were 106 firefighters killed while on duty.
- Fire killed more Americans than all natural disasters combined.
- 81 percent of all civilian fire deaths occurred in residences.
- 1.6 million fires were reported. Many others went unreported, causing additional injuries and property loss.
- Direct property loss due to fires was estimated at $11.3 billion.
- An estimated 31,000 intentionally set structure fires resulted in 305 civilian deaths.
- Intentionally set structure fires resulted in an estimated $755 million in property damage (USFA, 2007a, p. 2).

The USFA provides the following statistics on arson injuries and costs:

- An estimated 31,000 intentionally set structure fires occurred in 2006.
- Intentionally set fires in structures resulted in 305 civilian deaths.
- Intentionally set structure fires also resulted in $755,000,000 in property loss.
- 20,500 intentionally set vehicle fires occurred, a decrease of 2.4 percent from a year ago, and caused $134,000,000 in property damage, an increase of 18.6 percent from a year ago (USFA, 2007b, p. iii).

Water Accidents—Drowning

The CDC reports that the second leading cause of injury death for children under fifteen is drowning. Three times as many children who drown go to the emergency room for "nonfatal submersion injuries," and in many cases these "nonfatal drownings" can result in "brain damage that may result in long-term disabilities including memory problems, learning disabilities, and permanent loss of basic functioning (i.e., permanent vegetative state)" (CDC,

2008, para. 3). From 2005–2009, over 3,500 deaths from non-boating related drownings happened each year in the United States and nearly 350 drowned from boating accidents and one in five of these fatalities are children under fifteen and children ages one to four have the highest rates of drowning—most occurring in home swimming pools (CDC, 2012).

> My father is an EMT. I remember him coming home from work one day, a complete wreck. He had witnessed an infant who had fallen into her grandparent's indoor pool and drown to death. Ever since then, he became paranoid of my sister and I swimming. (twenty-one-year-old college junior).

The CDC reports the following as the major risk factors for drowning:

- Lack of barriers and supervision. Children under one year most often drown in bathtubs, buckets, or toilets. Among children ages one to four years, most drownings occur in residential swimming pools. Most young children who drowned in pools were last seen in the home, had been out of sight less than five minutes, and were in the care of one or both parents at the time. Barriers, such as pool fencing, can help prevent children from gaining access to the pool area without caregivers' awareness.
- Age and recreation in natural water settings (such as lakes, rivers, or the ocean). The percent of drownings in natural water settings increases with age. Most drownings in those over fifteen years of age occur in natural water settings.
- Lack of appropriate choices in recreational boating. In 2006, the U.S. Coast Guard received reports for 4,967 boating incidents; 3,474 boaters were reported injured, and 710 died. Among those who drowned, nine out of ten were not wearing life jackets. Most boating fatalities from 2006 (70 percent) were caused by drowning; the remainder were due to trauma, hypothermia, carbon monoxide poisoning, or other causes. Open motor boats were involved in 45 percent of all reported incidents, and personal watercraft were involved in another 24 percent.
- *Alcohol use.* Alcohol use is involved in up to half of adolescent and adult deaths associated with water recreation and about one in five reported boating fatalities. Alcohol influences balance, coordination, and judgment, and its effects are heightened by sun exposure and heat.
- *Seizure disorders.* For persons with seizure disorders, drowning is the most common cause of unintentional injury death, with the bathtub as the site of highest drowning risk (CDC, 2008, para. 3).

A research review of where children drown (published in the journal *Pediatrics*) found that roughly 60 percent of drownings happen among children under age five—with the overwhelming majority being boys (Brenner,

Trumble, and Smith, 2001). Nearly 88 percent of children were being supervised when they drowned—with a shocking 46 percent under parental supervision. The study by Brenner, Trumble, and Smith (2001) found that of reviewed drownings, a little over one-third happened in lakes, rivers, or ponds (37 percent), most happened in residential or community pools (39 percent), and 18 percent happened around the home (in baths, hot tubs, or buckets).

Those under five are at greater risk of drowning around the home, and older children (aged five to fourteen) are at greater risk of drowning in lakes, ponds, rivers, or other open bodies of water—with more than half of the older children (59 percent) choosing to be in the water. Another cause for concern is that parents and children often overestimate their swimming abilities and can easily get into trouble in the water.

ONGOING STRATEGIES TO IMPROVE THE ISSUE—HOW CAN WE MAKE THIS BETTER?

Athletics

Some of the adults who should be most keenly aware of the dangers of concussions from athletic injuries and hazing on sports teams are the following:

- coaches/assistant coaches/athletic directors/athletic trainers
- pediatricians and school nurses and team doctors
- parents
- children/students/athletic participants
- teachers and school staff and administrators
- referees

These interested stakeholders should be trained to look for signs of head injuries as well as hazing in sports, and they should work together to prevent and stop these problems from happening. Awareness of the above issues related to hazing and head injuries is a start, but schools and parents need to explore athletic policies and handbooks and encourage workshops to improve understanding of these issues.

For head injuries,

- Take seriously all blows to the head.
- Do not let players play after a head injury (to prevent second-impact syndrome).

• Parents, coaches, teachers, and all adults working with children need to be educated about the signs and symptoms of head injuries like concussions—and work to prevent them.

The CDC's fact sheet for coaches outlines the following steps that should be taken to prevent concussions (or all major head injuries), as well as steps to create an action plan if a young athlete is injured:

Preseason

• Ensure that players are medically evaluated and are in good condition to participate.
• Establish an action plan for handling concussions that occur. Be sure that other appropriate school officials know about your action plan and have been trained in its use.
• Explain your concerns and expectations about concussion and safe play to athletes and school officials.
• Ask if players have had one or more concussions during the previous season.
• Remind athletes to tell coaching staff if they suspect that a teammate has a concussion.
• Determine whether your school would consider conducting preseason baseline testing of brain function (neuropsychological assessment) in athletes.

During Season, Practice, and Game

• Monitor sports equipment for safety, fit, and maintenance.
• Enlist other teachers to monitor any decrease in grades that could indicate a concussion.
• Be sure appropriate staff is available for injury assessment and referrals for further medical care.
• Continue emphasizing with players, staff, and parents your concerns and expectations about concussion and safe play.
• Report concussions that occurred during the school year to appropriate school staff. This will help in monitoring injured athletes as they move to the next season's sports.

Postseason

• Work with appropriate staff to review injuries and illnesses that occurred during the season.

- Discuss any need for improvements in your action plan with appropriate health care professionals and school staff.
- Discuss with other staff any needs for better sideline preparations.

Create an Action Plan

To ensure that concussions are managed correctly, have an action plan in place before the season starts.

- Identify a health care professional to manage injuries during practice and competition.
- Fill out the pocket card enclosed in this kit and keep it with you on the field of play so that information about signs, symptoms, and emergency contacts is readily available.
- Be sure that other appropriate athletic and school staff and health care professionals know about the plan and have been trained in its use.

When a Concussion Occurs

If you suspect that a player has a concussion, implement your action plan by taking the following steps:

1. Remove the athlete from play. Learn how to recognize the signs and symptoms of concussion in your players. Athletes who experience signs or symptoms of concussion should not be allowed to return to play. When in doubt, keep the player out of play.
2. Ensure that the athlete is evaluated by an appropriate health care professional. Do not try to judge the severity of the injury yourself. Health care professionals have a number of different methods that they can use to assess the severity of concussion.
3. Inform the athlete's parents or guardians about the known or possible concussion and give them the fact sheet on concussion. Make sure they know that the athlete should be seen by a health care professional.
4. Allow the athlete to return to play only with permission from an appropriate health care professional. Prevent second impact syndrome by delaying the athlete's return to the activity until the player receives appropriate medical evaluation and approval for return to play (www. cdc.gov/ncipc/tbi/CGToolKit/Coaches_Guide.htm, para. 13–18).

Driver safety programs to prevent motor vehicle accidents, mandatory seat belt and helmet laws help, but in general these recommendations are useful for avoiding serious brain injuries like TBI:

- Seat belts: Make sure you always wear a seat belt every time you drive or ride in a motor vehicle and insist that your passengers wear them too. And never operate a vehicle under the influence of alcohol or other drugs.
- Car seats and booster seats for children: Make sure your child's car seat is properly installed and make sure the proper seat is used for your child's weight and height. Car seats should be rear facing until your child reaches twenty pounds; use booster seats after forty pounds and until your child is at least 4 ft. 9 in. tall. Buckle your child into the car using a child safety seat, booster seat, or seat belt (according to the child's height, weight, and age). Many police stations will assist parents in installing car seats for infants and children. Check with your local police station for help.
- Appropriate, well-fitting helmets: Make sure your child wears a helmet when playing any contact sport; riding a bike or any motorized device; skateboarding, rollerblading, or skating; playing baseball or softball; horseback riding; or skiing, sledding, or snowboarding.
- Safety-proofing: Safety-proof your home for children, which should include putting safety gates on stairs, installing window guards so children cannot fall out, keeping railings around porches and decks up to code, and using mulch or sand on playgrounds for softer landings.

Schools can work to develop awareness about these issues by working with the National Safe Kids Campaign website and the National Program for Playground Safety website. These sites have plans for teachers and have student handouts about playground, motor vehicle, and sports and recreation safety.

Importance of Helmets and New Concussion-reducing Technology

New helmets are coming onto the market that are designed to reduce the risk of concussions and other head injuries. For example, *Sports Business Daily* reported about a "new helmet [that] helps protect players from concussions." Recently, Harvard University quarterback Vin Ferrara designed one to be available in 2008. Also, the *Journal of Neurosurgery* reported that the Riddell's Revolution helmet "reduced concussions by 31 percent" (www.sportsbusinessdaily.com/index.cfm?fuseaction=sbd.main&ArticleID=116063&requesttimeout=500).

Preventing Bullying and Harassment on Athletic Teams

We need to pay attention and respond to all forms and reports of hazing, including examples like these, where younger players are treated differently than veteran players and are teased and harassed. Hazing can be very dangerous physically and emotionally, and adults must address and stop it. Because hazing tends to happen outside of adult awareness, little is written or known about the specific extent of the problem (e.g., statistics). More research needs to be conducted to determine the extent of hazing on sports teams and more specifics gathered about the experience.

As parents and teachers or individuals working with children and adolescents, we must pay attention to any of these signs and speak with the young person right away. There tends to be a culture of secrecy associated with hazing, so it will be difficult to get young people to speak out against the cruelty they experience. Still, it is important to push.

Adult supervision in locker rooms and other under-supervised places will help, as will teaching children to recognize the signs of hazing and encouraging them to tell a caring, responsible adult. Of course, children fear retaliation for reporting such incidents and that their participation on sports teams will be compromised. Coaches and parents, as well as other school personnel, need to set very clear guidelines that make it known that hazing and bullying are unacceptable.

Accidents

Preventing accidents is challenging. However, the same advocates will be able to help make children safer in the car, home, school, and around water—that is, adult care providers. These include parents, teachers, school administrators, law-enforcement officers, fire officials, lifeguards, day care providers, and other child-care workers (e.g., baby sitters).

Any person charged with the care of children must be made aware of the importance of seat belts, proper car seats, helmet wearing, careful supervision in high-risk areas (e.g., around water and busy streets), and fire- and water-safety plans. Schools should educate students and parents about safety in cars, on bicycles, around water, and in the event of fire. In some cases, policy changes and law enforcement vigilance are called for. Children should learn to swim and learn safety strategies at young ages and be supervised carefully.

Although some of the specific recommendations may differ for preventing motor vehicle and bicycle accidents, fire-related injuries, and drowning, there are a few general recommendations. The first is awareness of the specific risk factors, and the second is adult vigilance. Each of these accidents is among the leading causes of unintentional injury death for young people, and all need to be addressed in systematic ways by caring adults.

Protection from Motor Vehicle Accidents

Some preventative measures can be taken to reduce the chances of motor vehicle accidents. Consider the following:

- Make sure ability is not impaired by sleep deprivation, drugs (including over-the counter, cold medication, or alcohol), or emotional state.
- Make sure driving conditions are appropriate for driving.
- Take advantage of driver's education courses, and give young drivers as much supervised driving experience as possible.
- Have parents closely monitor their inexperienced adolescents' driving— making sure that conditions are safe, that they are not driving with too many distractions (friends, music, telephones), and when possible that they drive with competent adult supervision as they gain experience.
- Determine that car seats and booster seats for younger children are properly installed and maintained and that seat belts for younger riders are being used and fit appropriately.
- Increase awareness and intervention for other forms of auto-related accidents, such as children being backed over (install motion detectors on rear bumpers of cars), hit or run over by cars, or suffering heat stroke from being left in cars.
- Lobby for graduated driver's-licensing programs—particularly those that limit nighttime driving, have at least a six-month "learning period," and restrict the number of passengers until the driver has more experience.

Protection from Bicycle Accidents

The federal government has issued standards for helmet safety. Helmets should have a sticker from the Consumer Product Safety Commission (CPSC) indicating that it meets these standards. In addition to meeting helmet standards, helmets must fit properly—qualified personnel at bike stores or police stations can help determine if a helmet fits correctly if you are unsure. KidsHealth (2007) offers the following help in fitting helmets properly:

Once you have the right helmet, you need to wear it the right way so it will protect you. It should be worn level and cover your forehead. Don't tip it back so your forehead is showing. The straps should always be fastened. If the straps are flying, it's likely to fall off your head when you need it most. Make sure the straps are adjusted so they're snug enough that you can't pull or twist the helmet around on your head. There were many examples such as this one among our survey respondents: My friend's brakes gave out and she flipped over her bike damaging her teeth (college junior).

Having good bike equipment, including a well-fitting helmet (and checking before riding to make sure the helmet is in good repair), is also critical to preventing accidents such as the one in this example.

Children are also at risk of being hit by cars when riding their bicycles beside or in the road. Parents should be aware of where their children are riding and encourage them to stay away from busy and/or narrow-shouldered streets. The Bicycle Safe website (www.bicyclesafe.com) offers suggestions for how to avoid getting hit by cars while riding a bike, such as watching the way that you turn at a red light and signaling properly. The authors of the website also encourage getting a horn and a headlight, slowing down, and watching out for car doors opening as you ride by.

The KidsHealth website offers a section on bike safety for kids and gives reminders about road rules (e.g., stop and check traffic in both directions, cross at intersections, use proper hand signals), wear bright-colored clothing, make sure the bike is safe (e.g., working brakes, properly inflated tires, no loose clothing to get caught in bike chains, and so on).

The National Highway Transportation and Safety Association (NHTSA) reports that "universal bicycle helmet use by children aged 4–15 would prevent 39,000 to 45,000 head injuries, and 18,000 to 55,000 scalp and face injuries annually." The NHTSA reports that currently fourteen states have no state or local helmet laws (Arkansas, Colorado, Idaho, Indiana, Iowa, Minnesota, Mississippi, Nebraska, North Dakota, South Dakota, South Carolina, Utah, Vermont, and Wyoming). Lobbying for mandatory helmet laws for children under age eighteen in these states could help save lives and prevent harm to children—as will more consistent enforcement of helmet laws in the states that have them.

Protection from Fires

The U.S. Fire Administration (USFA) has a website for kids at www.usfa.dhs.gov/kids/flash.shtm. The site provides links to information about home fire safety, smoke alarms, and escaping from fires, as well as an opportunity to become a "junior fire marshal." The site also has more information on the USFA's fire prevention and safety campaigns. FireSafety.gov (2008), a website sponsored by the CDC, the CPSC, and the USFA, recommends the following to help prevent fires and to reduce injury and death in the event of a fire:

- Get a smoke alarm (approximately two-thirds of fire deaths happen in homes without working smoke alarms, which should be on every level of the house, both outside and inside of all sleeping areas, and properly installed and maintained).
- Make an escape plan (practice regularly, have two means of escape from every room, leave the house immediately, never open hot doors, create a meeting location away from the house that everyone knows about, and once you're out of the house, stay out).
- Practice fire safety (firesafety.org offers strategies for practicing safety in the home, such as bedroom, kitchen, and fireplace safety).

- Use fire sprinklers (studies by the USFA have demonstrated that sprinkler systems could perhaps have prevented thousands of injuries, saved thousands of lives, and prevented millions of dollars in damage to homes).

Protection from Drowning

Children should learn to swim and be taught water safety at a very young age—particularly if they live near or around water. Requiring young children to wear well-fitting life jackets whenever they are going to be playing in or near water can reduce the chances of drowning. The National Safe Kids Campaign's Splash into Safety program focuses on the following "water-safety wisdoms" for caregivers:

- Supervision—Designate a responsible adult to actively supervise kids around water.
- Environment—Ensure safe swimming environments by installing multiple layers of protection around pools and equipping all water recreation sites with appropriate signage and emergency equipment.
- Gear—Make sure the right safety gear is always used.
- Education—Teach children to swim and educate them about water safety (Safe Kids USA, 2004).

The Safe Kids Campaign also makes the following recommendations:

- Never leave a young child unsupervised in or around water, even for a moment.
- Never allow children to swim without adult supervision.
- Always designate a responsible adult to serve as the "water watcher"—a supervisor whose sole responsibility is to constantly observe children in or near the water.
- Supervisors should maintain continuous visual and auditory contact with children in or near the water, and should stay in close proximity (water-side) so that they can effectively intervene if an emergency situation should arise.
- Supervisors should not engage in distracting behaviors such as talking on the phone, preparing a meal, or reading.
- Supervisors should keep children who cannot swim within arm's reach at all times.
- While there is no specific recommended ratio of supervisors to child swimmers, the number of supervisors should increase when many children are swimming, younger or inexperienced swimmers are present, or the swimming area is large (Safe Kids USA, 2004, para. 4).

It is important for adults to remember that very young children can drown in only an inch or two of water, so always stay within reach of a very young child. The American Association of Pediatrics suggests the following safety tips for avoiding accidental drowning around the home:

* Empty all buckets, pails, and bathtubs completely after each use—do not leave them filled and unattended.
* Keep young children out of the bathroom unless they are closely watched. Teach others in the home to keep the bathroom door closed. Install a hook-and-eye latch or doorknob cover on the outside of the door.
* Never leave a child alone in a bathtub or in the care of another child, even for a moment.
* Use a rigid, lockable cover on a hot tub, spa, or whirlpool, or fence in all four sides as you would for a swimming pool.
* Set your water heater thermostat so that the hottest temperature at the faucet is 120°F to avoid burns.
* Throw away or tightly cover water or chemical mixtures after use.
* Watch children closely when they are playing near wells, open post holes, or irrigation or drainage ditches. Fill in empty holes or have fences installed to protect your child.
* Learn CPR and know how to get emergency help (American Academy of Pediatrics, 1994, para. 3).

A Few Words about Falls and Young Children

Young children are at risk of falling, particularly as they are learning to walk or still mastering such skills as climbing stairs. Using protective gates around fireplaces, stairs, and other dangerous places can help. Also, protective buffers on sharp-edged tables or other corners can prevent head injury during falls.

Children are also at risk of being injured from toys—with the majority of major injuries occurring from falls off of toys (Children's Health Encyclopedia, childrenscentralcal.org). Carefully monitor children on riding toys, and be sure that all toys are developmentally appropriate. Also, windows in children's rooms should be carefully latched to prevent youngsters from falling out. And finally, as children graduate from cribs to toddler or "big kid" beds, be sure to use safety devices to keep them from falling out of bed.

Motor Vehicle Accidents

Schools and communities need to invest in driver-training programs that teach young drivers defensive driving skills, the importance of wearing seat belts, and not to drive while under the influence of an impairing substance or to ride with anyone who is. As parents and/or adult caregivers, let adolescents know that they can be picked up any time, any place, no questions asked, to avoid their riding with unsafe peers. Also, communities and states need to invest in graduated driver's-licensing programs.

Bicycle Accidents

Carefully monitor where children can ride bikes. Make sure places are safe from cars and that children wear helmets at all times. Be sure that bicycles are in working order and that an adult is always supervising younger riders carefully.

Fire Safety

Children and adults need to be made aware of risks and safety strategies. Giving young children an opportunity to visit a fire station and see fire fighters in their uniforms can help (so they are not fearful if they see them during a fire). Also, children should know what to do in the event of a fire and practice—both at home and at school.

Water Safety

Attentive, skilled adult supervision is essential. Always watch children carefully when they are near any kind of water source—from the bathtub to a river (be sure when there are multiple adults that at least one is charged with watching all children). When possible, put up gates or fences to keep children out of water sources unless supervised. Invest in swimming lessons—encourage community recreation programs to offer reduced-rate or sliding-fee-scale (or even free) swimming lessons with qualified instructors.

WHAT CAN YOU DO RIGHT NOW?

Be sure that coaches, parents, and athletes have access to information about head injuries like concussions, traumatic brain injuries, and bullying and harassment on sports teams. Encourage schools to offer workshops on these topics for all the stakeholders.

- Athletics: Be on the look-out for signs of hazing on athletic teams (or other groups). Listen to what children and adolescents say to each other and when possible monitor children's interactions via text or phone.
- Accidents: Be vigilant around water—make sure there is always at least one adult paying attention to children in or near water. Make sure homes have sufficient smoke alarms and that children know what to do in the

event of a fire. Insist upon properly fitting helmet usage. Make sure young children have appropriate car seats and older children always wear seat belts.

Finally, cultivating a culture of mindfulness at a young age (as will be discussed in part 3), may help reduce accidents. Paying attention to what we are doing in the moment and encouraging children to be mindful of what they are doing each moment, may help keep all people safer.

TOP 3 TIPS FOR TEACHERS

1. Treat head injuries very seriously and seek medical attention immediately and limit following activity.
2. Provide information to students and parents about the dangers of accidents from water, fire, motor vehicles, etc. to encourage mindful attention paid to these dangers so they engage in preventative strategies such as helmet wearing, seat-belt and car seat usage, smoke alarms, and proper supervision around water.
3. Listen to what your students say to each other in their conversations about their experiences on athletic teams.

REFERENCES

Centers for Disease Control and Prevention (CDC). (1997). Sports-related recurrent brain injuries—United States. Morbidity and Mortality Weekly Report 46, no. 10: 224–27, www.cdc.gov/mmwr/preview/mmwrhtml/00046702.htm.
Dellinger, A., and Kresnow, M. (2010). Bicycle helmet use among children in the United States: the effects of legislation, personal and household factors. *NCBI*. Retrieved November 5, 2013, from http://www.ncbi.nlm.nih.gov/pubmed/20846554.
Guskiewicz, K. M., Weaver, N., Padua, D. A., and Garrett,W. E. (2000). Epidemiology of concussion in collegiate and high school football players. American Journal of Sports Medicine 28 (5): 643–50.
Harmon, K. G. (1999). Assessment and management of concussion in sports. American Family Physician 60 (3) (September 1): 887–92, 894.
Institute of Medicine. (2002). Is soccer bad for children's heads? Summary of the IOM workshop on neuropsychological consequences of head impact in youth soccer. Washington, DC: National Academy Press.
Kushner, D. S. (1998). Mild traumatic brain injury. Archives of Internal Medicine 158: 1617–24.
Lovell, M. R., M. W. Collins, G. L. Iverson, K. M. Johnston, and J. P. Bradley. (2004). Grade 1 or "ding" concussions in high school athletes. American Journal of Sports Medicine 32, (1): 47–54.
Powell, J. W. 2001. Cerebral concussion: Causes, effects, and risks in sports. Journal of Athletic Training 36 (3): 307–11.
Powell, J. W., and K. D. Barber-Foss. (1999). Traumatic brain injury in high school athletes. Journal of the American Medical Association 282: 958–63.
Seat Belt Safety, Seat Belt Laws. (n.d.). *Seat Belt Safety, Seat Belt Laws*. Retrieved November 5, 2013, from http://www.nsc.org/safety_road/DriverSafe.

Sosin, D. M., Sniezek, J. E., and Thurman, D. J. (1996). Incidence of mild and moderate brain injury in the United States, 1991. Brain Injury 10: 47–54.

Unintentional Drowning: Get the Facts (November 29, 2012). *Centers for Disease Control and Prevention.* Retrieved November 5, 2013, from http://www.cdc.gov/homeandrecreationalsafety/water-safety/waterinjuries-factsheet.html.

Zemper, E. D. (2003). Two-year prospective study of relative risk of a second cerebral concussion. American Journal of Physical Medicine and Rehabilitation 82 (September): 653–59.

ADDITIONAL RESOURCES

- Brain Injury Association of America (www.biausa.org): This organization provides information and resources to improve the quality of life for individuals with brain injuries.
- Centers for Disease Control and Prevention (www.cdc.gov/ncipc): This website has English and Spanish fact sheets and brochures on concussion and traumatic brain injury.
- Statistics on Sports Injuries
- Catastrophic Sports Injuries and Young People
- NCAA comparisons and statistics: www1.ncaa.org/membership/ed_outreach/health-safety/iss/Game_Comparison
- www.nata.org/jat/readers/archives/42.2/i1062-6050-42-2-toc.pdf
- National Center for Catastrophic Injury Research: www.unc.edu/depts/nccsi
- There are a number of places for more information on bullying, hazing, and protecting your child in athletics:

  - U.S. Department of Health and Human Services (http://mentalhealth.samhsa.gov/15plus/parent): This website provides tips for parents, grandparents, and caregivers, as well as for teachers and administrators.
  - GirlsHealth.gov (www.girlshealth.gov/bullying/index.htm): This website has information for these groups on bullying, cyberbullying, and hazing.

- The following groups were involved in the Centers for Disease Control's studies reported above:

  - American Academy of Pediatrics
  - American Association for Health Education
  - American College of Sports Medicine
  - American School Health Association
  - Association of State and Territorial Health Officials
  - Brain Injury Association of America
  - Institute for Preventative Sports Medicine

- National Association for Sport and Physical Education
- National Athletic Trainers' Association
- National Federation of State High School Associations
- National Safety Council
- North American Brain Injury Society
- University of Pittsburgh Medical Center Sports Medicine Concussion Program
- U.S. Department of Education

The websites of these agencies would be useful for more information on these topics too. References for CDC Fact Sheet cited above.

Chapter Seven

Alcohol and Other Drugs and the Developing Brain and Mind

Among the many goals of the developing brain is to regulate the critically important hormones and neurotransmitters within it that profoundly affect the experience of the mind. These substances affect how the cells within the brain communicate with one another and as a result affect thinking, emotions, and behavior. Psychoactive substances that will be discussed in this chapter act like these naturally occurring brain chemicals and disrupt the brain's natural functioning and attempts at regulating these levels of hormones and neurotransmitters. How serious is the problem? How do these substances work to affect the brain and mind? How do we prevent these problems?

According to an article summarizing the research on the impact of alcohol use on the developing adolescent brain "Studies conducted over the last eight years by federally financed researchers in San Diego, for example, found that alcoholic teenagers performed poorly on tests of verbal and nonverbal memory, attention focusing, and exercising spatial skills like those required to read a map or assemble a precut bookcase." The article cites several other studies that demonstrate similar cognitive issues for teenagers who abuse alcohol.

As Aaron White (assistant professor in psychiatry at Duke University who coauthored an important study in this area) told reporters at the *New York Times*, "There is no doubt about it now: there are long-term cognitive consequences to excessive drinking of alcohol in adolescence." Other popular recreational and prescription drugs also have an impact on the developing brain and mind. Not only in the short term does the use of substances impair the brain and mind, but longer term usage and abuse also impacts learning and memory and other areas of cognition.

77

NATURE OF THE ISSUE AND HOW IT AFFECTS CHILDREN

According to the 2012 National Survey on Drug Use and Health (NSDUH), "Nonmedical use of prescription medications is on the rise among U.S. teens, resulting in dangerous health consequences. In 2010 an estimated 66,517 emergency department (ED) visits involving nonmedical use of pharmaceuticals were made by adolescents aged 12 to 17, accounting for about two fifths (39 percent) of all drug related ED visits involving misuse or abuse of drugs in this age group" (DAWN, 2012, para 1).

In the 2013 report relying on national reports from Emergency Departments, the federal monitoring system, Drug Abuse Warning Network (SAMHSA.gov), reported that, "Marked findings of this report are (a) a 29 percent increase in the number of drug-related ED visits involving illicit drugs in the short term between 2009 and 2011; (b) simultaneous, short-term increases in the involvement of both illicit and licit stimulant-like drugs" (DAWN, 2013, para 2).

According to the 2013 report, the age group with the most drug-related ED visits was 18-20 year olds, followed closely by 21–24 year olds. Approximately 2.5 million ED visits each year are the result of drug abuse or misuse. The report states:

- "about 1.25 million ED visits, or 51 percent, involved illicit drugs;
- about 1.24 million, or 51 percent, involved nonmedical use of pharmaceuticals; and
- about 0.61 million, or 25 percent, involved drugs combined with alcohol.

In the long term, between 2004 and 2011, the annual overall number of ED visits attributable to drug misuse or abuse has risen steadily each year for a total increase of 52 percent, or about 844,000 visits. In the short term, between 2009 and 2011, ED visits involving overall misuse or abuse increased by 19 percent, or by about 400,000 visits over the two years. Almost half of the net increase in visits seen in the eight years from 2004 to 2011 occurred in the last two years of the period, 2009 to 2011.

In 2011, of the nearly 440,000 drug abuse–related ED visits made by patients aged twenty or younger more than 40 percent involved alcohol. DAWN estimated there were over 200,000 ED visits resulting from drug-related suicide attempts in 2011. Almost all involved a prescription drug or over-the-counter medication" (DAWN, p. 9).

In addition to these more purposeful abuses, there were also problematic rates of accidental drug ingestion by children. The report claimed that the preponderance of ED visits for accidental ingestion involved children aged five and under. "In 2011, out of a total of 113,634 visits, over 77,000 involved children in this age range. The rate of visits for accidental drug ingestion was about 25 times higher for children aged 5 and under than for adults: 318 visits per 100,000 children aged 5 and under compared with 13 visits per 100,000 population for the general adult population aged 21 or older. Pain relievers were the most common class of drugs involved in accidental ingestion among children aged 5 and under, appearing in 25 percent of visits" (DAWN, p. 10–11).

According to the annual Centers for Disease Control's Youth Risk Behavior Survey, over 23 percent of adolescents in grades 9–12 had used marijuana one or more times within the past thirty days of the survey, almost 7 percent had used some form of cocaine, over 11 percent had used inhalants, 2.9 percent used heroin, 3.8 percent used methamphetamines, and 3.6 percent used steroids at some point in their life. Students also smoked cigarettes (18 percent in the past thirty days) and drank alcohol (38.7 percent in the last thirty days) (Trends in the Prevalence, 2012).

Alcohol and other drug experimentation and use (including misuse of prescription drugs and illegal recreational drugs) in childhood and adolescence pose a double threat. Not only is the use of these substances harmful (and potentially lethal) to the developing brains and bodies of children and adolescents, but their combined use increases dangers resulting from poor decision making, such as in sexual promiscuity and driving/car accidents.

FIRST: THE DANGERS IN THEIR OWN RIGHT

Late childhood and early adolescence are critical periods for the developing body and brain. There is evidence to suggest that use of drugs, such as prescription drugs, alcohol, marijuana, and others, can have a long-term impact on learning and memory. In addition to causing physical and psychological dependence, adolescents and young adults can die from overdosing on many of these drugs.

Prescription drugs. Recently, a number of prescription drugs have been found to be among the drugs of choice for adolescents. And the federal government has shown a rise in Emergency Department visits for adolescents taking non-prescribed prescription medication. For example, Ritalin (a stimulant used to treat attention problems like attention deficit disorder) is abused by a variety of young people—sometimes they are trying to improve their performance in school or sporting events—much in the same way that caffeine is abused. Other drugs include depressants such as Valium, Xanax, and other sleep aids and narcotic/opiate pain-killers, such as OxyContin, Percodan, and Vicodin.

Sometimes adolescents have prescription drug parties where they take their parents' prescription drugs and put them in a giant bowl and take them—often washing them down with alcohol and using them with other recreational drugs such as marijuana. These "pharm parties" are extremely dangerous. At the time of writing this book, one of my students died from an overdose at one of these parties (KW).

In an article published by the Boston Public Health Commission titled "Teen Prescription Drug Abuse: An Invisible Epidemic," A. Raynor and J. Payne (2004) report that young women are about twice as likely to become dependent from abusing prescription medication as young men (with women between the ages of twelve and twenty-five showing increases in prescription drug abuse).

Sometimes abusing prescription medication may start because the user is trying to lose weight or reduce stress/anxiety, is experimenting or indulging curiosity, or is trying to fit in. It can be very difficult for teens to talk about prescription drug abuse. Also, young people may not realize the dangers of prescription drugs, mistakenly assuming that these drugs must be safer than street drugs as they are prescribed by doctors.

Caffeine: Legal for all. Caffeine is a popular and often-abused drug—but it is a drug, a stimulant that affects the brain and body by speeding up physiological processes. Caffeine affects sleep cycles. Children who drink caffeine products, such as energy drinks and sodas, may have difficulty sleeping, show signs and symptoms similar to attention deficit disorder, and have learning difficulties (as REM sleep cycles are critical to effective learning).

A position paper published in Monitor on Psychology called "A Sip into Dangerous territory" states, "Caffeine can stimulate immature neurological systems beyond children's ability to tolerate it, which can have serious effects," says APA Div. 43 (Family) President Terence Patterson, EdD, of the University of San Francisco. "Excessive caffeine use damages the attention capacity that children need to cooperate in play, family and school environments." Leading caffeine researcher Roland Griffiths, PhD, of Johns Hopkins University, deems the drug the most widely used mood-altering drug in the world, with usage far exceeding that of alcohol and nicotine. "Research has shown that the dose of caffeine delivered in a single can of soft drink is sufficient to produce mood and behavioral effects," he says. "Children who haphazardly consume caffeine are at risk for going through alternating cycles of withdrawal and stimulation" (O'Connor, 2001, para. 3).

Nicotine. Nicotine in any form is illegal to purchase until the age of eighteen. Nicotine's effects are quite well known (increased adult risk of cancer, heart attack, and stroke). Despite a gradual decline of tobacco use among adolescents, there are still over four million children between twelve and seventeen who smoke—a third of high school graduates are actively smoking (Leshner, 2005). The National Institute on Drug Abuse (NIDA) wrote of nicotine abuse and teens:

Nicotine is a powerfully addictive drug. Once your teen is addicted, it will be very difficult to quit. The cause of addiction is simple. Nicotine goes straight to the brain. The human brain has circuits that control feelings of pleasure. Dopamine—a brain chemical—contributes to the desire to consume drugs. Nicotine spikes an increase in dopamine. When your teen smokes, he or she inhales the nicotine. It goes quickly to the brain. In just 10 seconds, the pleasurable effects of smoking reach peak levels.

Within a few minutes, the pleasure is gone, and the craving for a cigarette begins a new cycle. A teen can easily get hooked on nicotine, although it takes much more effort to quit. Many kid smokers, they find it hard to stay away from the drug's effects (Leshner, 2005, para. 7–10).

NIDA has nicotine listed as one of the most addictive psychoactive substances. They list the following as the health concerns: Nicotine is highly addictive. The tar in cigarettes increases a smoker's risk of lung cancer, emphysema, and bronchial disorders. The carbon monoxide in smoke increases the chance of cardiovascular diseases. Secondhand smoke causes lung cancer in adults and greatly increases the risk of respiratory illnesses in children (NIDA, 2008c, para. 2).

New evidence suggests that people who start [smoking cigarettes] in their teens are more likely to become life-long smokers than those who first light up as adults . . . and when compared with nonsmoking peers, young smokers are more likely to be abusers of other drugs: In 2002, the National Survey on Drug Use and Health reported that roughly half (48.1 percent) of youths aged 12–17 who smoked cigarettes in the past month also used an illicit drug whereas only 6.2 percent of nonsmoking youths reported using an illicit drug in the past month (Zickler, 2004, para. 2).

Alcohol. The U.S. has had a love-hate relationship with alcohol. With prohibition in the early part of the twentieth century, to the repeal of this constitutional amendment years later (the only constitutional amendment to be repealed in our nation's history), so much of our culture is affected by alcohol. We socialize with alcohol. We celebrate with alcohol. We grieve with alcohol. We recognize the many health risks of alcohol—damage to our bodies and brains, as well as to unborn fetuses, and the impairments leading to accidents that occur under the influence, killing thousands of people per year. It is no wonder that young people experiment with this drug that is so prevalent and accepted in our culture. In addition, this drug targets powerful pleasure chemicals in our brains and lowers our stress/anxiety levels (albeit temporarily).

But alcohol is a central nervous system depressant—it is an illicit drug if you are under the age of twenty-one. It is dangerous. The National Institute on Alcohol Abuse and Alcoholism (NIAAA) reports that young people who drink are at higher risk of becoming victims of violent crime (e.g., rape, assault, and battery), having problems at school, being in car accidents, having unprotected sex, and developing drinking problems as adults.

As the young brain is developing rapidly during adolescence until about age twenty-five, alcohol can harm some of that development—the cognitive impairments are still being researched. The NIAAA provides a list titled "Warning Signs of a Drinking Problem":

Although the following signs may indicate a problem with alcohol or other drugs, some also reflect normal teenage growing pains. Experts believe that a drinking problem is more likely if parents notice several of these signs at the same time, if they occur suddenly, and if some of them are extreme in nature.

- Mood changes: flare-ups of temper, irritability, and defensiveness
- School problems: poor attendance, low grades, and/or recent disciplinary action
- Rebelling against family rules
- Switching friends, along with a reluctance to have parents get to know the new friends
- A "nothing matters" attitude: sloppy appearance, a lack of involvement in former interests, and general low energy
- Finding alcohol in a child's room or backpack, or smelling alcohol on his or her breath
- Physical or mental problems: memory lapses, poor concentration, bloodshot eyes, lack of coordination, or slurred speech (NIAAA, 2006, para. 3)

Other Popular Recreational Drugs

Marijuana. According to the results of the "Monitoring the Future Study" (a national survey of a sample of students in grades eight, ten, and twelve), marijuana use has been steadily declining since the late 1990s, but the study still shows that nearly 40 percent of those in twelfth grade had used the drug at least once. The National Survey on Drug Use and Health reported in 2006 that 14.8 million people aged twelve or older used marijuana at least once a month.

Marijuana can be smoked (in a carved-out cigar called a blunt, a pipe, a water bong, or a cigarette/joint) or ingested (in bread or brownies or in tea). As R. A. Nicoll and B. N. Alger in their *Scientific American* article titled "The Brain's Own Marijuana" write, Marijuana is a drug with a mixed history. Mention it to one person, and it will conjure images of potheads lost in a spaced-out stupor. To another, it may represent relaxation, a slowing down of modern madness. To yet another, marijuana means hope for cancer patients suffering from the debilitating nausea of chemotherapy, or it is the promise of relief from chronic pain.

The drug is all these things and more, for its history is a long one, spanning millennia and continents. It is also something everyone is familiar with, whether they know it or not. Everyone grows a form of the drug, regardless of their political leanings or recreational proclivities. That is because the brain makes its own marijuana, natural compounds called endocannabinoids (after the plant's formal name, Cannabis sativa) (2004, para. 1).

Because marijuana targets cannabinoid receptors of the brain, it is believed that the parts of the brain that have more of these receptors are affected most by marijuana use. These areas include pleasure centers and coordination centers for memory, concentration, perception of time, and movement. The drug affects these areas and also dopamine neurons that affect pleasure and reward. NIDA reports that there is an "addictive potential" from long-term marijuana use, as well as "an association between chronic marijuana use and increased rates of anxiety, depression, suicidal ideation, and schizophrenia" (NIDA, 2008b). Earlier ages of first use tend to lead to greater problems in these areas (see NIDA, 2008b www.drugabuse.gov/Infofacts/marijuana.html).

Other health (emotional and physical) risks from marijuana smoking are as follows (according to NIDA):

Effects on the Heart

One study found that an abuser's risk of heart attack more than quadruples in the first hour after smoking marijuana. The researchers suggest that such an outcome might occur from marijuana's effects on blood pressure and heart rate (it increases both) and reduced oxygen-carrying capacity of blood.

Effects on the Lungs

Numerous studies have shown marijuana smoke to contain carcinogens and to be an irritant to the lungs. In fact, marijuana smoke contains 50 to 70 percent more carcinogenic hydrocarbons than tobacco smoke. Marijuana users usually inhale more deeply and hold their breath longer than tobacco smokers do, which further increases the lungs' exposure to carcinogenic smoke. Marijuana smokers show dysregulated growth of epithelial cells in their lung tissue, which could lead to cancer; however, a recent case-controlled study found no positive associations between marijuana use and lung, upper respiratory, or upper digestive tract cancers. Thus, the link between marijuana smoking and these cancers remains unsubstantiated at this time.

Nonetheless, marijuana smokers can have many of the same respiratory problems as tobacco smokers, such as daily cough and phlegm production, more frequent acute chest illness, a heightened risk of lung infections, and a greater tendency toward obstructed airways. A study of 450 individuals found that people who smoke marijuana frequently but do not smoke tobacco have more health problems and miss more days of work than nonsmokers. Many of the extra sick days among the marijuana smokers in the study were for respiratory illnesses.

Effects on Daily Life

Research clearly demonstrates that marijuana has the potential to cause problems in daily life or make a person's existing problems worse. In one study, heavy marijuana abusers reported that the drug impaired several important measures of life achievement including physical and mental health, cognitive abilities, social life, and career status. Several studies associate workers' marijuana smoking with increased absences, tardiness, accidents, workers' compensation claims, and job turnover (NIDA, 2008b, para. 9–12).

Cocaine. Cocaine is a central nervous system stimulant that mimics the brain's natural pleasure chemicals. Cocaine can be snorted or eaten in powdered form, injected, or smoked (in the form of crack freebasing). There is some concern that adolescent use of cocaine "could alter the normal growth of brain regions affected by cocaine, specifically the reward system" (Catlow and Kirstein, 2007, para. 1). However, researchers Catlow and Kirstein note that "very little is known about how repeated exposure to drugs of abuse during adolescence alters normal brain development" (2007, para. 2). Yet consistent research has shown that the impact of drugs of abuse on adolescent rats' brains is far more severe than it is on adult rats' brains.

The negative impact of cocaine can depend somewhat on the way it is used. For example, if smoked, damage to the lungs and throat and other respiratory problems can occur. If snorted, loss of smell, chronic nosebleeds, difficulty swallowing or speaking, and general irritation to the nose and throat can occur. Intravenous use can result in easier overdose, track marks, and possibly allergic reactions. Some of the general effects of cocaine are heart attacks, respiratory failure, strokes, and seizures. Large amounts can cause bizarre and violent behavior. In rare cases, sudden death can occur on the first use of cocaine or unexpectedly thereafter.

The short-term physiological effects of cocaine include constricted blood vessels; dilated pupils; and increased temperature, heart rate, and blood pressure. Large amounts (several hundred milligrams or more) intensify the user's high, but may also lead to bizarre, erratic, and violent behavior. These users may experience tremors, vertigo, muscle twitches, paranoia, or, with repeated doses, a toxic reaction closely resembling amphetamine poisoning. Some users of cocaine report feelings of restlessness, irritability, and anxiety.

In rare instances, sudden death can occur on the first use of cocaine or unexpectedly thereafter. Cocaine-related deaths are often a result of cardiac arrest or seizures followed by respiratory arrest. Use of cocaine in a binge, during which the drug is taken repeatedly and at increasingly high doses leads to a state of increasing irritability, restlessness, and paranoia. This may result in a full-blown paranoid psychosis, in which the individual loses touch with reality and experiences auditory hallucinations (CocaineDrugAddiction.com, 2008, para. 5).

Interestingly, new drug research suggests that adolescents are much more likely to "become addicted and relapse more easily than adults because developing brains are more powerfully motivated by drug-related cues" (APA, 2008, para. 2). Comparing adolescent rats to adult rats, researchers have found that the adolescents were more likely to continue to seek out cocaine than adults—and even after they quit using, they were more apt to start using again when given the chance than the adult rats (Brenhouse and Andersen, 2008).

Other stimulants. Amphetamines, methamphetamine, and Ritalin are all stimulants. Methamphetamine (typically in a form of powder or clear crystals that can be dissolved, then snorted, smoked, or injected) is made in illegal labs from easily available items such as battery acid, antifreeze, and drain cleaner. The other two are typically prescribed medications. Ritalin is prescribed for attention deficit disorder. They share similar effects with other stimulants in that they speed the user up—including heart rate, blood pressure, energy level, and so forth—and when abused, they share similar effects to cocaine (in high doses) and caffeine (in low doses).

"Bath salts." According to the National Institute on Drug Abuse "the term 'bath salts' refers to an emerging family of drugs containing one or more synthetic chemicals related to cathinone, an amphetamine-like stimulant found naturally in the Khat plant." We have seen a rise in the use and abuse of these "bath salts" used similarly as methamphetamine.

Inhalants. Inhalants exist all around the home and even in schools. These often toxic substances, such as glues, gasoline, nitrous oxide, and some household cleaners, are sniffed or huffed using a bag, rag, or balloon (in the case of nitrous oxide). These drugs are typically classified into three basic categories:

Solvents include

- Certain industrial or household products, such as paint thinner, nail polish remover, degreaser, dry-cleaning fluid, gasoline, and glue
- Some art or office supplies, such as correction fluid, felt-tip marker fluid, and electronic contact cleaner

Gases include

- Some household or commercial products, such as butane lighters, propane tanks, whipped cream dispensers, and refrigerant gases

- Certain household aerosol propellants, such as those found in spray paint, hair spray, deodorant spray, and fabric protector spray
- Medical anesthetic gases, such as ether, chloroform, halothane, and nitrous oxide

Nitrites include

- Cyclohexyl nitrite (found in substances marketed as room deodorizers)
- Amyl nitrite (used for medical purposes)
- Butyl nitrite (previously used in perfumes and antifreeze but now an illegal substance) (NIDA for Teens, 2008, para. 3–5)

According to NIDA, nearly twenty-three million young people admitted to having used inhalants at least once—with numbers increasing. These chemicals are widely available, making them an easy high for youngsters. Because these chemicals are often toxic, they have very harmful effects on the developing brain, including harming nerve cells and fibers as well as memory centers. Regular abusers may show harm not only to the brain but also to the heart, liver and kidneys, and muscles.

Steroids. Anabolic steroids are substances that mimic the hormone testosterone. These should not be confused with corticosteroids, which are prescribed to treat skin reactions and reduce inflammation. Anabolic steroids can be taken orally (in pill form) or injected, typically intramuscularly. Some abusers "stack" their use by taking two or more different kinds at once—or "pyramid" doses in weekly cycles—alternating doses. The numbers of adolescents using steroids according the Monitoring the Future survey ranges from 2.5 percent of eighth graders to 4 percent of high school seniors.

The effects can range from increased acne on the face and body to increased body and facial hair (on girls and boys). Boys may develop breasts. Liver and heart complications can occur. Another serious concern is what is called "'roid rages," which are violent, angry outbursts. In my career as professor and counselor (KW), I have encountered a handful of adolescents abusing steroids—all with consistent stories of these angry, uncontrollable outbursts—sometimes resulting in fighting or hurting another person.

One student was removed from college for such outbursts and threats made against fellow students. In all cases, the reasons were the same—to "get bigger and stronger." In some cases, they were athletes wanting to get better, but in more cases, they were young men wanting to enhance their appearance. Because hormone levels are fluctuating in adolescents and the brain is developing and working toward finding a balance of hormones, adding synthetic hormones to the mix is profoundly problematic for developing bodies and brains.

Club Drugs

Ecstasy/MDMA. The scientific name for Ecstasy is 3,4-methylenedioxyme-thamphetamine. It is created in illicit labs with no safety controls, so it is difficult to know what is in the pills. Sometimes these pills involve all kinds of other compounds from caffeine to amphetamine to cocaine. Drops in usage were seen earlier in this decade with a huge drop among high school seniors (from 11.7 percent to 5.4 percent between 2001 and 2005) according to the NIDA "High School and Youth Trends" survey.

Ecstasy has been called a "rave" or "party" or "dance" drug because it gives users the energy to dance for hours. Some people experience an increase in body temperature (some have died from overheating as MDMA interferes with the body's ability to regulate temperature). In addition, some experience dehydration, sweating, chills, anxiety, agitation, muscle tension, confusion, depression, sleep problems, clenching of teeth, blurry vision, fainting, and increases in heart rate and blood pressure (NIDA for Teens, 2008). Ecstasy has also been called the "love drug" because users claim they feel closer to other people. Adolescents are more likely to have more and unprotected sex with several partners under the influence of such a drug.

There are other club drugs such as "Special K" (ketamine), LSD, and GHB (gamma hydroxy butyrate). Surveys of adolescent drug use have shown an increase in GHB abuse in the United States since 1992. Like ketamine, GHB was initially used as an anesthetic (ketamine for veterinary use). It is a colorless, tasteless, and odorless liquid but can be available in powder or capsule/pill form. Users claim that it causes a euphoric feeling, increased sex drive, and lowered inhibitions. Some side effects are nausea/vomiting, dizziness, drowsiness, and seizure activity. In higher doses, loss of consciousness, irregular or lowered respiration, tremors, or even coma can occur.

Opiates: Opium, heroin. In 2006 over a half a million people aged twelve and older had used heroin at least once in the past year (www.monitoringthefuture.org). Opium and heroin can both be injected or smoked. As with the other drugs mentioned, adolescent use of these substances is particularly problematic as users' brains and bodies are still developing, and abuse of these chemicals may result in lifelong health consequences. Some more immediate consequences are poor mental functioning, shallow breathing, difficulty moving (heavy feeling in extremities), dry mouth, and infections at injection sites; more serious effects include infectious diseases from sharing needles (HIV/AIDS, hepatitis), collapsed veins, or fatal overdoses.

The 2007 Monitoring the Future study showed that there was a slight increase (from 0.2 to 0.3 percent) among eighth graders, and use without a needle among twelfth graders increased from 0.6 percent to 1 percent. Vicodin and OxyContin, which are both opiates in prescription pill form, were reportedly used by 2.7, 7.2, and 9.6 percent of eighth, tenth, and twelfth graders, respectively.

SECOND: POOR DECISION MAKING MADE POORER

New research on the adolescent brain has shown that the way teenagers make decisions can be fundamentally different from the way adults make decisions. Some cutting-edge research comparing the adolescent and adult brains using fMRI technology has shown not only that different areas of the brain are involved in making decisions about potentially harmful ideas (e.g., swimming with sharks), but it takes teenagers longer to arrive at these sometimes dangerous decisions (e.g., swimming with sharks is a good idea) (Baird and Bennett, in Powell, 2006).

The brain is still growing, maturing, and developing until about age twenty-five, researchers are finding, and part of that maturation is an improved ability to make complex decisions. Drugs affect decision making in teens two ways. First, teens tend to make poorer decisions than adults about risk-taking behaviors—including those about drugs. Second, teens will likely make even poorer decisions under the influence of drugs, like the above, that lower inhibitions and reduce cognitive functioning. This means that decisions about sexual activity, driving, and other risk-taking behaviors will be worsened under the influence.

THIRD: POOR DRIVING MADE POORER

Drinking and drugging while driving. The National Highway Traffic Safety Administration (NHTSA) reported that in 2010 over ten thousand people died in alcohol-related car crashes. And according to the National Survey on Drug Use and Health:

- Approximately 10.3 million people twelve years of age or older drove under the influence of illegal drugs in 2012.
- In 2009 of those killed in car accidents, 18 percent of drivers tested positive for at least one illegal drug.
- In 2006, an estimated 13.3 percent of persons age twelve and older drove under the influence of an illicit drug or alcohol at least once in the past year. This percentage has dropped since 2005, when it was 14.1 percent. The 2006 estimate corresponds to 32.8 million persons.
- Driving under the influence of an illicit drug or alcohol was associated with age. In 2006, an estimated 7.3 percent of youth age sixteen drove under the influence. This percentage steadily increased with age to reach a

peak of 31.8 percent among young adults age twenty-two. Beyond the age of twenty-two, these rates showed a general decline with increasing age.

- Also in 2006, among persons age twelve and older, males were nearly twice as likely as females (17.6 percent versus 9.3 percent) to drive under the influence of an illicit drug or alcohol in the past year.

In recent years, drugs other than alcohol that act on the brain have increasingly been recognized as hazards to road traffic safety. Some of this research has been done in other countries or in specific regions within the United States, and the prevalence rates for different drugs vary accordingly. Overall, the research indicates that marijuana is the most prevalent illegal drug detected in impaired drivers, fatally injured drivers, and motor vehicle crash victims. Other drugs also implicated include benzodiazepines, cocaine, opiates, and amphetamines (NIDA, 2008a, para. 5–6).

Drugs impair cognition for drivers, and inexperienced drivers need all of their mental focus to be able to drive effectively. Car accidents are one of the leading causes of death for adolescents, and drugs (including alcohol) have been found to play a major role in these accidents. The Monitoring the Future survey found that 13 percent of twelfth graders reportedly drove under the influence of marijuana in the two weeks before the survey. When inexperienced teen drivers get behind the wheel, we are all in danger.

The upside is that the percentage of teens dying in drugged-driving crashes has declined 63 percent since 1982 and 10 percent since 2000 (NHTSA, 2007). But the numbers are still unacceptable as nearly six thousand teenage drivers die in car crashes each year, and over a third of them are under the influence of alcohol or other drugs.

Certainly all adults in our society should be concerned about teenage substance use and abuse. However, some key advocates should be included when attempting to reduce drug use and abuse in the home, school, or larger community. First are educators—teachers, parents, administrators, school counselors, community program workers. Second are social workers or other community agencies working with youth as caseworkers and Child Protective Services agents. Third are emergency personnel, such as EMTs and police officers, and other health care providers, such as physicians and nurses.

Community members, including school board members, and shop owners who sell nicotine and alcohol products, as well as pharmacy workers and owners, must make sure that youngsters do not have access to different prescription and over-the-counter substances that are potentially problematic.

ONGOING STRATEGIES TO IMPROVE THE ISSUE—HOW CAN WE MAKE THIS BETTER?

Alcohol is the most widely abused substance and is illegal for children under age twenty-one.

Here are some ways, according to the NIAAA to prevent teen abuse of alcohol:

Monitor Alcohol Use in Your Home. If you keep alcohol in your home, keep track of the supply. Make it clear to your child that you don't allow unchaperoned parties or other teen gatherings in your home. If possible, however, encourage him or her to invite friends over when you are at home. The more entertaining your child does in your home, the more you will know about your child's friends and activities.

Connect with Other Parents. Getting to know other parents and guardians can help you keep closer tabs on your child. Friendly relations can make it easier for you to call the parent of a teen who is having a party to be sure that a responsible adult will be present and that alcohol will not be available. You're likely to find out that you're not the only adult who wants to prevent teen alcohol use—many other parents share your concern.

Keep Track of Your Child's Activities. Be aware of your teen's plans and whereabouts. Generally, your child will be more open to your supervision if he or she feels you are keeping tabs because you care, not because you distrust him or her.

Develop Family Rules about Youthful Drinking. When parents establish clear "no alcohol" rules and expectations, their children are less likely to begin drinking. Although each family should develop agreements about teen alcohol use that reflect their own beliefs and values, some possible family rules about drinking are

- Kids will not drink alcohol until they are twenty-one.
- Older siblings will not encourage younger brothers or sisters to drink and will not give them alcohol.
- Kids will not stay at teen parties where alcohol is served.
- Kids will not ride in a car with a driver who has been drinking.

Set a Good Example. Parents and guardians are important role models for their children—even children who are fast becoming teenagers. Studies indicate that if a parent uses alcohol, his or her children are more likely to drink as well. But even if you use alcohol, there may be ways to lessen the likelihood that your child will drink. Some suggestions include:

- Use alcohol minimally, responsibly, or not at all—children notice when their parents have had too much to drink.

- Don't communicate to your child that alcohol is a good way to handle problems. For example, don't come home from work and say, "I had a rotten day. I need a drink."
- Let your child see that you have other, healthier ways to cope with stress, such as exercise; listening to music; or talking things over with your spouse, partner, or friend.
- Don't tell your kids stories about your own drinking in a way that conveys the message that alcohol abuse is funny or glamorous.
- Never drink and drive or ride in a car with a driver who has been drinking.
- When you entertain other adults, serve alcohol-free beverages and plenty of food. If anyone drinks too much at your party, make arrangements for them to get home safely.
- Don't support teen drinking.
- Help your child build healthy friendships.
- Encourage healthy alternatives to alcohol (NIAAA, 2006, p. 15–18).

Raynor and Payne (2004, p. 2) recommend the following tips for parents in their article about teen prescription drug abuse:

- Parents can make a difference in their child's life!
- Be sure to listen more to your child.
- Spend time together.
- Share your family values.
- Talk to your child, but not at them.
- Agree to disagree and be respectful.
- Help build your child's self-esteem.
- Keep the lines of communication open.

Caffeine and Nicotine. Eliminate altogether or severely limit any intake of caffeine in the diets of young people. Schools should avoid having any caffeinated beverages available in vending machines or in the cafeteria and should treat caffeinated beverages like other drugs in school—they are not allowed without parental consent. Adults need to be educated (as do young people) about the problems associated with caffeine. Unlike caffeine, which is not illegal for youth to consume, nicotine is illegal for those under age eighteen to use. All nicotine products, including gums, patches, and chewing tobacco, are illegal—but also dangerous—as are cigarettes, the obvious and most widely abused form of nicotine. Talk to kids about the dangers of smoking—preventing them from even trying tobacco is the best form of prevention. But once they start, getting kids to quit is also important. Groups like the NIDA are looking at strategies to help adolescents quit effectively.

Alcohol. The National Institute on Alcohol Abuse and Alcoholism of the National Institutes of Health has a helpful guide for parents about ways to talk with their children about alcohol. They recommend several points in their publication (available for download at http://pubs.niaaa.nih.gov/ publications/MakeADiff_HTML/makediff.htm#TakingAction). The highlights of their recommendations are as follows:

• Develop an open, trusting relationship.
• Encourage open conversations; ask open-ended questions and control your emotions if you don't agree or if something your child says upsets you.
• Try not to lecture but to have a sharing of ideas. Ask your child what he or she thinks or knows about alcohol and share the facts about alcohol, providing good reasons to avoid drinking.

The above recommendations can help young people stay away from all other drugs too—not just alcohol. Teenagers need to be carefully monitored by caring adults who give them increased freedom as they earn it by showing responsible behavior. If you as an adult suspect a problem with a young person with any drug, get help as soon as possible. The school's counselor or psychologist, the child's physician, or another health care professional can be helpful in determining the extent and nature of any drug problem.

Parents and prescription drugs. Carefully monitor any prescription medication you own. Count the number of tablets and destroy any unused portions, particularly of narcotic medication.

Cocaine. The best approach is prevention, using many of the same strategies as for the other drugs. Signs of a cocaine problem can be sudden weight loss, sleep disturbance, attention problems, and extreme energy followed by periods of exhaustion. Cocaine dependency is typically treated using psychological interventions rather than medical or pharmaceutical ones. Because many cocaine-addicted young people also are addicted to alcohol, treating the alcohol dependence medically to avoid harmful withdrawal is important.

Seeking medical treatment for a young person struggling with addiction is very important. The bottom line is that to break the pattern of addiction, adolescents or young adults need to change their lifestyles and patterns of behavior—as well as their friends and associates. This can be very challenging and requires a great deal of support.

WHAT CAN YOU DO RIGHT NOW?

Preventing All Drug Problems: Some General Rules

• Educate yourself about the effects of different drugs and drugs that are growing in popularity. Reading this chapter is a good first step in what you can do now.

- Talk to your child openly about drugs and their effects and ask pointed, specific, nonjudgmental questions about drug use in school and who is using what— continue to ask these questions periodically.
- Monitor conversations, texts, etc. for information about who is doing what. Learn some of the current jargon (ask children about these terms).
- Ask to see any survey that the school has conducted about students' self-reported drug use to find out the nature of the drugs used and the extent of use.
- Stress healthy alternatives and provide options for healthy opportunities through athletics, music, art, etc.
- Be sure to explain healthy ways to reduce stress and interact socially without alcohol or other drugs. Model this behavior for your child/children.
- Pay attention to your child's friends. Who are they? What do they do? Where do they go? What do they do there?

OPEN PARENTING/OPEN TEACHING: THE BASIC ABCS

*A*uthentic and open. Parents and teachers—in fact, any adult interested in raising healthy and safe youngsters—need to be authentic—that is, real. As we invite young people to be open and honest with us, they need to know that they can trust us, no matter what. Parents wonder, should I be honest about my own experiences as a child or adolescent? It depends on the message you want to send.

*B*ut don't flinch. Keep emotions in check when listening—and ask good questions to get children to be honest about what they are doing, with whom they are doing it, and their fears and concerns. You must stay neutral to achieve this kind of safe space where kids will talk with you honestly.

*C*are no matter what. Make it clear to your child that you care, and no matter what he or she tells you, your feelings will not change—you will still care, unconditionally. Your child must believe this—and you must convey this level of care. Make it clear, for example, by saying to your child, "I'll pick you up any time, any place, no questions asked."

TOP 3 TIPS FOR TEACHERS

1. Listen to student conversations and what they say about drugs and encourage students to talk to you about their experiences and fears about alcohol and other drugs. Let students know that they can talk to you and while you cannot keep secrets, you will listen and help give advice about people to talk to for more help.

2. Educate yourself about the different drugs—particularly the ones that are most often mentioned or indicated as problematic in surveys of student usage—so you can talk openly with students about these drugs and encourage them to get help as needed.

3. Be on the lookout for changes in behavior, attitude, academic work/ performance among your students and determine whether this could be a result of drug use or abuse (e.g., hyper-stimulated behavior or depressed or difficulty concentrating, etc.).

REFERENCES

American Psychological Association (APA). (2008). Rat study suggests why teens get hooked on cocaine more easily than adults. ScienceDaily. www.sciencedaily.com/releases/2008/04/ 080421133021.htm (accessed June 13, 2008).

Brenhouse, H. C., and Andersen, S. L. (2008). Delayed extinction and stronger reinstatement of cocaine conditioned place preference in adolescent rats, compared to adults. Behavioral Neuroscience 122(2): 460–65.

Butler, K. (2006, July 24). The Grim Neurology of Teenage Drinking—New York Times. *The New York Times—Breaking News, World News & Multimedia*. Retrieved June 14, 2013, from http://www.nytimes.com/2006/07/04/health/04teen.html?pagewanted=all&_r=0.

Catlow, B. J., and Kirstein, C. L. (2007). Cocaine during adolescence enhances dopamine in response to a natural reinforcer. Neurotoxicology 29 (1): 57–65.

CocaineDrugAddiction.com. 2008. Cocaine addiction facts: What is cocaine addiction? Co-caineDrugAddiction.com. www.cocainedrugaddiction.com.

Drug Misuse or Abuse-Related Emergency Department Visits Involving Nonmedical Use of Pharmaceuticals Vary by Gender among Older Adolescents (2012, November 30). *Drug Abuse Warning Network*. Retrieved June 11, 2013, from www.samhsa.gov/data/spotlight/ spot089-adolescent-nonmedical-rx-use.pdf

Drug Abuse Warning Network, 2011: National Estimates of Drug-Related Emergency Depart-ment Visits. (2013, May 1). *http://www.samhsa.gov/*. Retrieved June 1, 2013, from www.samhsa.gov/data/2k13/DAWN2k11ED/D.

Leshner, A. I. (2005). Parents: Nicotine is a real threat to your kids. National Institute on Drug Abuse. www.drugabuse.gov/Published_Articles/Nicotinethreat.html (accessed June 12, 2008).

National Highway Traffic Safety Administration (NHTSA) (2007). Traffic safety annual as-sessment: Alcohol-impaired driving fatalities. www-nrd.nhtsa.dot.gov/Pubs/811016.pdf (ac-cessed October 22, 2008).

National Institute on Alcohol Abuse and Alcoholism (NIAAA). (2006). Make a difference—talk to your child about alcohol. http://pubs.niaaa.nih.gov/publications/MakeADiff_HTML/ makediff.htm#TakingAction (accessed June 12, 2008).

National Institute on Drug Abuse (NIDA) (2008a). NIDA InfoFacts: Drugged Driving. www.drugabuse.gov/Infofacts/driving.html.

———. (2008b). NIDA InfoFacts: Marijuana. www.drugabuse.gov/Infofacts/marijuana.html.

———. (2008c). Tobacco/nicotine.www.drugabuse.gov/drugpages/nicotine.html.Fact Sheets. (2012, April 1). *National Institute on Drug Abuse*. Retrieved November 4, 2013, from http:// www.drugabuse.gov/category/product-format/fact-sheetswaterinjuries-factsheet.html.

Nicoll, R. A., and Alger, B. N. (2004). The brain's own marijuana. Scientific American (No-vember), www.sciam.com/article.cfm?id=0008F53F-80F7-119B-80F783414B7F0000 (ac-cessed June 12, 2008).

NIDA for Teens. (2008). Inhalants. NIDA for Teens. http://teens.drugabuse.gov/facts/ facts_inhale1.asp.

O'Connor, E. (2001). A sip into dangerous territory. Monitor on Psychology 32 (5): www.apa.org/monitor/jun01/dangersip.html (accessed June 12, 2008).

Office of Applied Studies (OAS) (2007). A day in the life of American adolescents: Substance use facts. October 18. www.oas.samhsa.gov/2k7/youthFacts/youth.pdf (accessed June 14, 2008).

Powell, K. (2006). Neurodevelopment: How does the teenage brain work? Nature 442 (August 23): 865–67.

Raynor, A., and Payne, J. (2004). Teen prescription drug abuse: An invisible epidemic. Boston Public Health Commission. www.bphc.org/reports/pdfs/report_193.pdf (accessed June 12, 2008).

Trends in the Prevalence of Marijuana, Cocaine, and Other Illegal Drug Use National YRBS: 1991–2011 (2012, January 1). *Trends in the Prevalence of Marijuana, Cocaine, and Other Illegal Drug Use National YRBS: 1991–2011.* Retrieved January 1, 2013, from www.cdc.gov/healthyyouth/yrbs/pdf/us_drug_.

Zickler, P. (2004). Early nicotine initiation increases severity of addiction, vulnerability to some effects of cocaine. NIDA Notes 19 (2) (July), www.nida.nih.gov/NIDA_notes/ NNvol19N2/Early.html (accessed June 13, 2008).

NIAAA RECOMMENDED RESOURCES

- Join Together, One Appleton St., 4th Floor, Boston, MA 02116 Phone: (617) 437-1500. Website: www.jointogether.org. Serves as a national resource center for communities across the nation that are working to prevent alcohol and other drug abuse.

- National Council on Alcoholism and Drug Dependence (NCADD). 22 Cortlandt St., Ste. 801, New York, NY 10007. Phone: (800) NCA-CALL (622-2255) (toll-free; twenty-four-hour affiliate referral). Website: www.ncadd.org. Provides educational materials on alcohol abuse and alcoholism as well as phone numbers for local NCADD affiliates, who can supply information about local treatment resources.

- National Institute on Alcohol Abuse and Alcoholism. 5635 Fishers Ln., MSC 9304, Bethesda, MD 20892-9304. Phone: (301) 443-3860. Website: www.niaaa.nih.gov. Makes available free informational materials on many aspects of alcohol use, alcohol abuse, and alcoholism.

- Substance Abuse and Mental Health Services Administration. National Drug Information Treatment and Referral Hotline. Phone: (800) 662-HELP (4357) (toll-free). Website: www.findtreatment.samhsa.gov. Provides information, support, treatment options, and referrals to local rehab centers for drug or alcohol problems. Operates twenty-four hours a day, seven days a week.

Chapter Eight

Physical Illness and Obesity

According to the Centers for Disease Control and Prevention which tracks data on childhood obesity annually, "childhood obesity has more than doubled in children and tripled in adolescents in the past 30 years. . . . In 2010, more than one third of children and adolescents were overweight or obese." (CDC Facts, para, 1–3). Inadequate nutrition, fast and processed food, and overreliance on sodas and other high-calorie beverages instead of healthy water and food, as well as a lack of physical activity, have resulted in an epidemic of overweight children. Obesity causes significant and serious health risks and problems.

How extensive is the obesity problem in the United States? What does it mean to be overweight? What can be done to improve it? How does obesity affect the brain and mind?

NATURE OF THE ISSUE AND HOW IT AFFECTS CHILDREN

Generally "overweight" is defined as follows: "excess body weight for a particular height from fat, muscle, bone, water or a combination of these factors." (Krebs et al., 2007). And "obesity" is defined as "having excess body fat" (Krebs et al., 2007).

Childhood obesity poses one of the greatest long-term health threats to our nation's children. Part of the growing trend of obesity is the result of poor nutrition, and part is from inactivity. The number one killer of adult Americans is that "silent killer" of heart disease—and obesity contributes to risk factors for heart disease.

The best predictor of adult obesity is childhood obesity, as a recent, comprehensive study following nearly ten thousand children into adulthood found (Freedman, Khan, and Dietz, 2001). There are ways that adult caregivers can reduce the risk later in life for children and adolescents. The primary ways are through the promotion of a healthy diet low in fat and processed foods, plenty of healthy water (and reduction of sodas or other drinks high in sugar), reduced stress/anxiety, involvement in food decisions (shopping, preparation, and so forth), and regular exercise.

How Extensive Is the Obesity Problem in the United States?

The Centers for Disease Control and Prevention reported the following based on their 2011 Youth Risk Behavior Survey that among high school students in the United States:

- *Obesity.* 13 percent were obese (students who were > 95th percentile for body mass index, based on sex- and age-specific reference data from the 2000 CDC growth charts).
- *Unhealthy Dietary Behaviors.* 5 percent did not eat fruit or drink 100 percent fruit juices during the seven days before the survey.

  - 6 percent did not eat vegetables during the seven days before the survey. (1)
  - 11 percent drank a can, bottle, or glass of soda or pop three or more times per day during the seven days before the survey. (2)

- *Physical Inactivity.* 14 percent did not participate in at least sixty minutes of physical activity on any day during the seven days before the survey. (3)

  - 71 percent were physically active at least sixty minutes per day on less than seven days during the seven days before the survey. (3)
  - 48 percent did not attend physical education (PE) classes in an average week when they were in school.
  - 69 percent did not attend PE classes daily when they were in school.
  - 32 percent watched television three or more hours per day on an average school day.
  - 31 percent used computers three or more hours per day on an average school day. (Taken verbatim from http://www.cdc.gov/healthyyouth/yrbs/pdf/us_obesity_combo.pdf.)

How Does Obesity Affect the Brain and Mind?

Many recent studies have shown diminished capacity of the brain among obese people. A report summarizing research of John Gunstad and his colleagues at Kent State University found that "obesity subtly diminishes memory and other features of thinking and reasoning even among seemingly healthy people, an international team of scientists reports. At least some of these impairments appear reversible through weight loss. Researchers also report one likely mechanism for those cognitive deficits: damage to the wiring that links the brain's information-processing regions" (Raloff, 2011, para. 1). The good news is that weight loss does seem to have a positive impact on regaining cognitive losses.

A study done with children was not as optimistic about the reversibility. The research showed that obese children with metabolic syndrome (those with insulin resistance, pre-diabetes, high blood pressure, high belly fat, and high triglycerides scored as much as 10 percent lower than non-obese children on cognitive tasks related to learning and memory. The researchers reported "Adolescents with MetS showed significantly lower arithmetic, spelling, attention, and mental flexibility and a trend for lower overall intelligence" (Yau, Castro, Tagani, Tsui, and Convit, 2012). The evidence supports the notion that obesity and its health complications are associated with poorer brain and mind function.

How Does Obesity Affect Children in the Short Term?

The CDC examined a great deal of published research on the short term ramifications of obesity on children and found the following immediate health effects for children and adolescents:

- High cholesterol
- High blood pressure
- Risk factors for cardiovascular disease
- Pre-diabetes
- Bone and joint problems
- Sleep apnea
- Social problems (ostracized)
- Poor self esteem
- Psychological problems

The CDC also summarized research findings and reported that children and adolescents who were obese were in the longer term more likely to be obese adults and therefore had the following long term risks:

- Heart disease
- Type 2 diabetes
- Stroke
- Several types of cancer
- Osteoarthritis

ONGOING STRATEGIES TO IMPROVE THE ISSUE – HOW CAN WE MAKE THIS BETTER?

Childhood obesity. Why should we care so much about childhood obesity? Children who are obese risk long-term health risks (such as heart disease), but they can also develop more immediate health problems such as type 2 diabetes, high blood pressure, asthma/respiratory or other breathing problems, early puberty, skin infections, eating disorders, sleep disturbances/disorders, and even liver disease. In addition, children who are extremely overweight are often at higher risk of being bullied and harassed and suffer lowered self-esteem, leading to learning problems and/or depression.

Childhood obesity and activity. Physical activity is an important factor in reducing health risks from obesity in children, and it is important for brain health as discussed in chapter1. Parents and other caregivers can help children by promoting physical fitness, reducing television and video game (and other sedentary activities) time, and encouraging outside active play.

For example, a study published in 2006 by Gable, Chang, and Krull found "Children who watched more television and ate fewer family meals were more likely to be overweight for the first time at spring semester of third grade. Children who watched more television, ate fewer family meals and lived in neighborhoods perceived by parents as less safe for outdoor play were more likely to be persistently overweight. Child aerobic exercise and opportunities for activity were not associated with a greater likelihood of weight problems. . . . This study supports theories regarding the contributions of television watching, family meals and neighborhood safety to childhood weight status" (2006, 53)

Clearly, the results of this study and the several that these authors reviewed show that parents need to reduce the television watching of their children. They also need to work to create time for family meals—and to learn about nutrition to provide healthy meals.

What Can Be Done to Improve It?

The Centers for Disease Control and Prevention recommend the following to stem the tide of the obesity epidemic:

- Better health education
- More PE and physical activity programs
- Healthier school environments
- Better nutrition services (The Obesity Epidemic and the United States, 2012)

We feel this is insufficient. The nature of physical activity in schools is limited and in many schools students obtain excuses to opt out. Students who often need the activity the most are the ones who are bullied most in gym class and do whatever they can to avoid the bullying, so have many excuses to avoid playing. Students need to learn physical activities that they can use for a lifetime, not just dodgeball and volleyball or floor hockey. They need to learn how to move their bodies, lift weights, stretch, do yoga, get their heart rates elevated (what this feels like and how to monitor it), and even just brisk walking. Schools can learn from successful voluntary exercise programs. What makes people go to the classes at the gym? Fun energizing music, good instruction, challenging but achievable moves, a feeling of accomplishment, and a feeling of community.

Physical education classes in school can be really traumatizing places for obese children (or even mildly overweight children). This is a space of bullying and teasing for those who are not as athletic as others. So, those who need the exercise end up getting the least as they are not passed the ball or included in the team sports games because they are not as coordinated or talented. We must work to find physical activities that meet the needs of all children. If a child is injured or disabled, activities should be found that a child can do successfully that still require movement and cardiovascular work.

Schools should monitor children's activity outside of school the way that many elementary programs monitor how much reading children do at home (through reports and journals, etc.). School physical education programs should assign "homework" for exercise that involves the whole family— helps them make a plan for activity (e.g. walking each day, setting goals for distance, setting times aside for exercise each day, and keeping track).

WHAT CAN YOU DO RIGHT NOW?

Obesity. The Mayo Clinic (2008, para. 27) recommends the following to prevent childhood obesity:

- Schedule yearly well-child visits. Take your child to the doctor for well-child checkups at least once a year. During this visit, the doctor measures your child's height and weight and calculates his or her body-mass index (BMI). Increases in your child's BMI or in his or her percentile rank over one year, especially if your child is older than four, is a possible sign that your child is at risk of becoming overweight.
- Set a good example. Make sure you eat healthy foods and exercise regularly to maintain your weight. Then, invite your child to join you.

- Avoid food-related power struggles with your child. You might unintentionally lay the groundwork for such battles by providing or withholding certain foods—sweets, for instance, as rewards or punishments. As a general rule, foods aren't recommended for behavior modification in children.
- Emphasize the positive. Encourage a healthy lifestyle by highlighting the positive—the fun of playing outside or the variety of fresh fruit you can get year-round, for example.
- Emphasize the benefits of exercise apart from helping to manage their weight. For example, it makes their heart, lungs, and other muscles stronger. If you foster your child's natural inclination to run around, explore, and eat only when hungry—not out of boredom—a healthy weight should take care of itself.
- Be patient. Many overweight children grow into their extra pounds as they get taller.
- Realize, too, that an intense focus on your child's eating habits and weight can easily backfire, leading a child to overeat even more, or possibly make him or her more prone to developing an eating disorder.

THREE TIPS FOR TEACHERS AND PARENTS

1. Demand regular physical activity and education in school. As many school districts are cutting physical education (PE) time and recess/play time, children are getting far less of the activity they need in a given week. As parents and teachers or other concerned community members, lobby for more time spent in PE courses and after-school intramural activities and organized athletics. Children should strive toward sixty minutes of physical activity per day. As most of their waking time is spent in schools, this is the logical place for this to happen.

2. Take children for basic yearly physicals (as teachers talk to parents to encourage annual physicals) to determine BMI and nutritional intake. After improving the amount and quality of physical education and activity for children, be sure to measure the fitness and BMI of children to determine if there is some improvement in the overall fitness and reduction in obesity levels in your school. As parents, you can work with your child's pediatrician to determine a plan and measure progress toward lowered BMI and increased levels of fitness.

3. Examine absences and test scores. Perhaps one of the best and easiest measures of improved nutrition and fitness is examining changes in absenteeism in schools as well as test scores. If children are living and eating better, they will feel better, be healthier, and attend school more regularly—and ultimately they will perform better.

REFERENCES

Bliss, R. M. (2004). Survey links fast food, poor nutrition among U.S. children. U.S. Department of Agriculture Research Service.www.ars.usda.gov/is/pr/2004/040105.htm (accessed June 12, 2008).

CDC—Obesity, Facts, Adolescent and School Health. (2013, February 19).*Centers for Disease Control and Prevention.* Retrieved June 17, 2013, from http://www.cdc.gov/healthyyouth/obesity/fa

CNN. 2000. U.N.: Poor nutrition could handicap 1 billion children. CNN. March 20. http://archives.cnn.com/2000/WORLD/europe/03/20/nutrition.report (accessed June 12, 2008).

Freedman, D. S., L. K. Khan, and W. H. Dietz. 2001. Relationship of childhood obesity to coronary heart disease risk factors in adulthood: The Bogalusa heart study. Pediatrics 108: 712–18.

Gable, Sara, Yiting Chang, and Jennifer L. Krull, 2007. Television watching and frequency of family meals are predictive of overweight onset and persistence in a national sample of school-aged children. Journal of the American Dietetic Association 107 (1): 53–61.

Kozol, Jonathan. 2006. Shame of the nation: The restoration of apartheid schools in America. New York: Random House.

Krebs, N. F., Himes, J. H., Jacobson, D., Nicklas, T. A., Guilday, Styne, D. Assessment of child and adolescent overweight and obesity. *Pediatrics* 2007;120:S193–S228.

Mahoney, C. R., H. A. Taylor, R. B. Kanarek, and P. Samuel. 2005. Effect of breakfast composition on cognitive processes in elementary schoolchildren. Psychology and Behavior 85: 635–45.

Mayo Clinic. 2008. Childhood obesity. MayoClinic.com. www.mayoclinic.com/health/childhood-obesity/DS00698.

PHS Group. 2005. Drinking water provision boosts brainpower in Welsh primary schools. PHS Waterlogic. www.phs.co.uk/waterlogic/1444.html.

Raloff, J. (2011, April 23). Obesity messes with the brain | Nutrition | Science News. *Science News.* Retrieved June 13, 2013, from http://www.sciencenews.org/view/generic/id/71742/description/Obesity_messes_with_the_brain

The Obesity Epidemic and U.S. Students. (2012, January 1). *The Obesity Epidemic and U.S. Students.* Retrieved January 1, 2013, from www.cdc.gov/healthy.

Yau, P., Castro, M., Tagini, A., Tsui, W., & Convit, A. (2012, September 2). Obesity and Metabolic Syndrome and Functional and Structural Brain Impairments in Adolescence . *Pediatrics* . Retrieved June 13, 2013, from http://pediatrics.aappublications.org/content/early/2012/08/28/peds.2012 0324.

Chapter Nine

Mental Illness in Children

Mental illness originates in the brain and affects the experience of the mind and affects the rest of the body, family, school, community, and world. Problems with certain brain functions or brain areas can result in psychological difficulties such as anxiety or depression. Hormonal or neurotransmitter levels in the brain can also affect mental health and well-being as these brain chemicals are largely responsible for how we feel and our emotional experiences. What happens when these levels are disrupted or problematic? What happens when areas of the brain are affected in such a way that children feel depressed, anxious, or dangerously aggressive?

We're a nation that lives for numbers and statistics to guide our opinions. If we're told that 5 million U.S. children have some type of mental illness that significantly interferes with daily life, we can murmur about it and agree, that's a lot of mentally ill children. Another number is 20 percent, which is the number of children per year diagnosed with a mental illness. Again, that's a pretty big number (Hasler, 2011).

What are the reasons for such growth in mental illness? There are many theories, such as problems in areas of the brain or in brain development, insufficiency or over stimulation of hormone or neurotransmitter levels in the brain, damaged DNA, toxins in the air and water, poor parenting, genetic predisposition, uncertainty and insecurity in our society, poor schools, and a society that is egotistical and not concerned about meeting the needs of its young.

Serious mental illness impacts large numbers of our nation's youth. Mental illness is treatable and the best outcomes occur with early identification and intervention. We can avoid the tragic and costly consequences of unidentified and untreated mental illness in youth by taking action. We can and should do far better for our nation's youth.

105

NATURE OF THE ISSUE AND HOW IT AFFECTS CHILDREN

Children's mental health problems are real, common, and treatable. Although one in five children has a diagnosable mental health problem, nearly two-thirds of them get little or no help.

The Facts

1. About 13 percent of youth aged 8–15 live with mental illness severe enough to cause significant impairment in their day-to-day lives. This figure jumps to 21 percent in youth aged 13–18.
2. Half of all lifetime cases of mental illness begin by age fourteen and three-quarters by age twenty-four. Early identification and intervention improve outcomes for children, before these conditions become far more serious, more costly and difficult to treat.
3. Despite the availability of effective treatment, there are average delays of eight to ten years between the onset of symptoms and intervention—critical developmental years in the life of a child. In our nation, only about 20 percent of youth with mental illness receive treatment.
4. Unidentified and untreated mental illness is associated with serious consequences for children, families, and communities. Approximately 50 percent of students aged fourteen and older with mental illness drop out of high school—the highest dropout rate of any disability group.
5. Over 90 percent of those who die by suicide have a mental illness. Suicide is the third leading cause of death for youth aged 15–24; more youth and young adults die from suicide than from all natural causes combined.
6. Over 70 percent of youth in state and local juvenile justice systems have mental illness, with at least 20 percent experiencing severe symptoms. At the same time, juvenile facilities fail to adequately address the mental health needs of youth in their custody.
7. Untreated mental health problems can disrupt children's functioning at home, school, and in the community. Without treatment, children with mental health issues are at increased risk of school failure, contact with the criminal justice system, dependence on social services, and even suicide (NAMI, 2013).

Parents and family members are usually the first to notice if a child has problems with emotions or behavior. Your observations, along with those of teachers and other caregivers, can help determine whether you need to seek help for your child.

The following signs may indicate the need for professional help. Symptoms in children vary depending on the type of mental illness, but some of the general symptoms include

1. Abuse of drugs and/or alcohol
2. Inability to cope with daily problems and activities
3. Changes in sleeping and/or eating habits
4. Excessive complaints of physical ailments
5. Defying authority, skipping school, stealing, or damaging property
6. Intense fear of gaining weight
7. Long-lasting negative moods, often accompanied by poor appetite and thoughts of death
8. Frequent outbursts of anger
9. Changes in school performance, such as getting poor grades despite good efforts
10. Loss of interest in friends and activities they usually enjoy
11. Significant increase in time spent alone
12. Excessive worrying or anxiety
13. Persistent nightmares or night terrors
14. Persistent disobedience or aggressive behavior
15. Frequent temper tantrums
16. Hearing voices or seeing things that are not there (hallucinations)
17. Decline in school performance
18. Poor grades despite strong efforts
19. Repeated refusal to go to school or to take part in normal activities
20. Hyperactivity or fidgeting
21. Depression, sadness, or irritability (National Institute of Mental Health, 2013)

Parents and teachers are on the front lines of daily interactions with children and youth. The list mentioned above is not extensive but comprehensive enough that it should raise a red flag that there may be an evolving problem. Mental illness never develops overnight. It is a slow decline into illness. Children exhibit these symptoms over long periods of time, sometimes years in the making.

Educators and parents need to be keen observers for any types of behavioral or cognitive changes that occur when a child is highly stressed or challenged or in situations where the response to a stimuli is much more extensive or radical than it should be for the child or for a child that age. Teenagers typically overreact to situations because of some of their cognitive beliefs. However, if the response is irrational or blown out of proportion, one must document it and see if there are patterns developing around certain issues.

A variety of causes may be responsible for mental illness in children and adolescents: environmental factors such as fearful experiences or chronic stress or worry or even lack of oxygen in areas with high pollution or high elevation; physical/medical factors such as medical illness or medication side-effects or anemia or asthma; substance abuse (particularly stimulants or withdrawal from depressants); genetic factors (family history); and brain chemistry (higher levels of certain neurotransmitters such as cortisol, hormones that stimulate the neuronal connections such as estrogen/testosterone).

There are several different types of mental disorders that can affect children and adolescents, including

- Anxiety disorders: Children with anxiety disorders respond to certain things or situations with fear and dread, as well as with physical signs of anxiety (nervousness), such as a rapid heartbeat and sweating.
- Attention-deficit/hyperactivity disorder (ADHD): Children with ADHD generally have problems paying attention or concentrating, can't seem to follow directions, and are easily bored and/or frustrated with tasks. They also tend to move constantly and are impulsive (do not think before they act).
- Disruptive behavior disorders: Children with these disorders tend to defy rules and often are disruptive in structured environments, such as school.
- Pervasive development disorders: Children with these disorders are confused in their thinking and generally have problems understanding the world around them.
- Eating disorders: Eating disorders involve intense emotions and attitudes, as well as unusual behaviors associated with weight and/or food.
- Elimination disorders: Disorders that affect behavior related to using the bathroom. Enuresis, or bed-wetting, is the most common of the elimination disorders.
- Learning and communication disorders: Children with these disorders have problems storing and processing information, as well as relating their thoughts and ideas.
- Affective (mood) disorders: These disorders involve persistent feelings of sadness/depression and/or rapidly changing moods, and include depression and bipolar disorder.
- Schizophrenia: This disorder involves distorted perceptions and thoughts.
- Tic disorders: These disorders cause a person to perform repeated, sudden, involuntary (not done on purpose), and often meaningless movements and sounds, called tics (WEBMD, 2013).

This is but a short list of what constitutes mental health challenges for youth and children. These disorders come in different degrees and are often seen over a continuum of difficulty. Some of these disorders may co-exist with others and in so doing may confuse the adults or the educators working with the student. Co-morbidity is very common and it is key that specific observations be made to ensure that the criteria for the disorder is clearly met and documented over a period of time. The Diagnostic Manual of Mental Health Disorders is an excellent reference for the specific criteria.

ONGOING STRATEGIES TO IMPROVE THE ISSUE—HOW CAN WE MAKE IT BETTER?

The basics for a child's good mental health can be summarized easily with the following:

1. Give children unconditional love. Children need to know that your love does not depend on their accomplishments.
2. Nurture children's confidence and self-esteem. Praise and encourage them. Set realistic goals for them. Be honest about your mistakes. Avoid sarcasm.
3. Encourage children to play. Play time is as important to a child's development as food. Play helps children be creative, develop problem-solving skills and self-control, and learn how to get along with others.
4. Enroll children in an after school activity, especially if they are otherwise home alone after school. This is a great way for kids to stay productive, learn something new, gain self-esteem, and have something to look forward to during the week. Or check in on children after school if they are home alone. Children need to know that even if you're not there physically, you're thinking about them, and interested in how they spent their day and how they'll spend the rest of it.
5. Provide a safe and secure environment. Fear can be very real for a child. Try to find out what is frightening him or her. Be loving, patient, and reassuring, not critical.
6. Give appropriate guidance and discipline when necessary. Be firm, but kind and realistic with your expectations. The goal is not to control the child, but to help him or her learn self-control.
7. Communicate. Make time each day after work and school to listen to your children and talk with them about what is happening in their lives. Share emotions and feelings with your children.
8. Get help. If you're concerned about your child's mental health, consult with teachers, a guidance counselor or another adult who may have information about his or her behavior. If you think there is a problem, seek professional help. Early identification and treatment can

help children with mental health problems reach their full potential (Mental Health America, 2000).

WHAT CAN WE DO NOW?

The treatment most often used for children with mental illness is medication. There are many cautions when using medications for children. Many of the clinical trials for the medications were done on adults and not children. Parents and educators need to be watchful of the many side effects of medication. Sometimes the cure is worse than nothing at all.

Many children have been known to benefit from play therapy, art therapy, animal therapy, and psychotherapy. It is important to remember the age of the child and their ability to process their own behaviors and thoughts.

Medication targets areas of the brain responsible for the hormones or neurotransmitters responsible for the problems. For example, classes of drugs used to treat major depression are the Selective Serotonin Reuptake Inhibitors (SSRI) and work by affecting the reabsorption of serotonin in the brain—this affects the balance of serotonin in the brain and leads to mood improvement. These classes of drugs are sometimes also used to treat anxiety. ADHD medication works to target stimulant neurotransmitters in the brain (dopamine and norepinephrine) and also restore balance to these as they are important for memory formation, arousal, and attention. In addition researchers have also shown that ADHD drugs target areas responsible for attention, impulse control, and decision making in the front of the brain.

Many mentally ill children just live the nightmare on a daily basis without having an idea of what is going on. Parents need to be able to explain to children what is happening with their bodies or their minds. Communication and understanding of the illness will go a long way in helping the child to recognize the triggers and events that create or happen prior to an episode.

Without treatment, many mental disorders can continue into adulthood and lead to problems in all areas of the person's adult life. People with untreated mental disorders are at high risk for many problems, including alcohol or drug abuse, and (depending on the type of disorder) violent or self-destructive behavior, even suicide.

When treated appropriately and early, many children can fully recover from their mental disorder or successfully control their symptoms. Although some children become disabled adults because of a chronic or severe disorder, many people who experience a mental illness are able to live full and productive lives.

REFERENCES

Hasler, N. (2011). Mental Illness in Children. Retrieved August 9, 2013, from http://justthink. org/about/mental-illness-and-children/? gclid=CNSb0cHN8bgCFSdk7AodIx8A5w.

Mental Health America (2000). What every Child needs for Good Mental Health. Retrieved August 9, 2013, from http://www.nmha.org/farcry/go/information/get-info/children-s-mentalhealth/what-every-child-needs-for-good-mental-health.

National Institute of Mental Health.(2013). Recognizing Mental Health Problems in Children. Retrieved August 9, 2013, from http://www.nmha.org/farcry/go/information/getinfo/children-s-mental-health/recognizing-mental-health-problems-in-children.

National Association of Mental Health (2013). Children's Mental Health Fact Sheet. Improving Lives: Avoiding Tragedies.

WebMD (2013). Mental Illness in Children. Retrieved August 9, 2013, from http://www. webmd.com/mental-health/mental-illness-children.

Chapter Ten

Violence and Abuse

Chronic stress from abuse and fear of violence and experiences of aggression affect the brain and are affected by the brain. The brain controls our behavior including our fears and aggression and violence. Bruce Perry explains the neurobiology of aggression and violence as follows:

> "The most dangerous children are created by a malignant combination of experiences. Developmental neglect and traumatic stress during childhood create violent, remorseless children. This is characterized by sensitized brainstem systems (e.g., serotonergic, noradrenergic and dopaminergic systems). Dysregulated brainstem functions (e.g., anxiety, impulsivity, poor affect regulation, motor hyperactivity) are then poorly modulated by poorly organized limbic and cortical neurophysiology and functions (e.g., empathy, problem-solving skills) which are the result of chaotic, undersocialized development. This experience-based imbalance predisposes to a host of neuropsychiatric problems and violent behavior."

Violence is a complex part of American culture and education that is controlled by the brain and mind and affects the brain and mind. The ongoing discussion on how to prevent violence in our society has been in existence since the War of Independence. America was built out of war. There seems to be a fighter instinct built into the brains and minds of American citizens. The right to protect oneself and bear arms is in the U.S. Constitution. However, a study published in 2013 in the *American Journal of Medicine* "debunk[s] the historic belief among many people in the United States that guns make a country safer. . . . On the contrary, the US, with the most guns per head in the world, has the highest rate of deaths from firearms, while Japan, which has the lowest rate of gun ownership, has the least" (Boseley, 2013).

Guns do not make us safer and put us and our children at higher risk of gun violence.

In the twenty-first century it is time to re-examine the way we deal with school violence; bullying; and physical, emotional, and sexual abuse. The attacks and assaults upon children and adolescents are at all-time highs. Gun violence in the United States is higher than in any other country, and we have more guns per person than any other country. How problematic is violence for children in this country? What can we do to prevent children from becoming victims of violence?

Today's children are faced with new challenges. They are faced with a variety of critical issues that are inherited from their parents, families, and communities. Millions of children, in this country as well as worldwide, lack safe homes, food to eat, quality childcare, and safe communities that protect them despite their lack of proper emotional, psychological, and social modeling. Research suggests this generation will live longer than their parents—if they do not fall victim to accidents or violence at the hands of others or themselves.

In this century we have better ways to eat, live, and be productive, yet we are losing a generation of children due to a lack of family values, bonding, and nurturance. Instead, we are creating a massive group of children who do not have the coping mechanisms to communicate, interact appropriately, or solve problems in a constructive and proactive way.

Since the turn of the century, we have seen an increase in runaways, prostitution, sexual offenders, violent crimes, homelessness, and vehicular accidents for juveniles. A similar increase has also been seen in the use of guns and weapons, school shootings, bullying and victims, and poverty.

In one of the wealthiest countries in the world we have a subculture that exists within our communities. It is one full of subversive-dysfunctional individuals who are only trying to find a place to survive. Often thrown into a life of survival at an early age and with a lack of knowledge, education, or support systems, they create ways they believe will enable them to attain what they believe they deserve, are entitled to, or will allow them to survive another day and not die.

Our society has coined the terms "latch-key kids," "throw-away kids," and "garbage kids." Imagine knowing as a child or adolescent that this is how society sees you. It brings forth a variety of emotions and rage. We often wonder why children act out against mainstream society. We treat these so-called "juvenile delinquents" as lesser than us, take away their ability to be productive, and enclose them in lock-up facilities, while never reaffirming to them that they are a worthwhile individual. Once a juvenile has embarked on a life of violence, it is very difficult to change him or her (mostly him) or that he will be rehabilitated. The end result for many of these children and juveniles is early death, or a life of incarceration. Not a great choice!

What are the kinds of violence that children are most likely to experience? How prevalent is this? What can be done to prevent it?

NATURE OF THE ISSUE AND HOW IT AFFECTS CHILDREN

Children are vulnerable individuals because they rely on adults for many of their basic needs. They do not have the capacity to go to work, shop for food, pay bills, and so forth. They are also vulnerable because their young brains and minds are developing at such a rapid rate, and their brain development is profoundly affected by their early experiences. As a teacher or parent, it is crucial that you become aware of the possible warning signs that a child is being abused. One factor that should trigger concern for a child is a change in the child's functioning, whether it is physical (soiling), behavioral (active to passive), or emotional (weepy or moody).

The following are factors that adults need to be aware of that may be in play for an abused child. There are several environmental factors worth noting that may place a child at risk:

- social isolation
- poverty
- domestic violence
- stress from financial problems, unemployment, inadequate housing, illness, and lack of child care
- parent with history of abuse
- parents who are emotionally immature, impulsive, or needy
- poor parenting skills and lack of knowledge about child development
- unrealistic parental expectations of a child
- disruptions to the early bonding process between parent and child
- a child who is difficult to care for (learning disabled, physically disabled, emotionally disturbed, or a behavior problem) (American Psychological Association, 2003)

There is a series of indicators of physical, sexual, and emotional abuse and neglect. The important component is to recognize the behaviors and warning signs. Most states have a list that is used to gauge whether or not abuse is occurring. This list is not exhaustive, and the author highly suggests that you consult your local or state handbook on child abuse and neglect to have the checklist as a guide in your assessment of the situation.

Physical abuse refers to non-accidental physical injury to a child. With physical abuse, look for a pattern or series of events. Be aware of frequent occurrences that alone may seem to have a reasonable explanation but, when taken as a whole, cause concern. Some of the indicators may be extensive bruises, burns, frequent complaints of injuries, sleep problems, headaches, enuresis, substance abuse, regression, social withdrawal, delinquency, stealing, running away, truancy, school leaving, anxiety, depression, guilt, suicidality, anger, aggression, and tantrums.

Sexual abuse refers to any sexual contact with a child or the use of a child for someone else's sexual pleasure. The signs of sexual abuse include a sudden and inexplicable fear of people and places, a severe interest in or avoidance of "all things of a sexual nature," nightmares, depression, withdrawal, secretiveness, delinquency, aggression, and suicidal behavior. Another large indicator is verbalization or physical reenactment of sexual activities, especially in a young child. Sexually abused children may not be able to say that they were sexually abused; instead, they often use words like dirty, damaged, and hurt to express pain.

Neglect refers to a failure to provide a minimum degree of care in supplying a child with adequate food, clothing, shelter, education, or medical care, resulting in physical, cognitive, or emotional impairment or danger of impairment. Some of the signs are failure to thrive, poor hygiene, poor health, malnutrition, rocking back and forth for self-soothing, begging or stealing food, crying easily, impaired socialization, falling asleep in class, being troublesome at school, lying, anxiety, withdrawal, hostility, anger, illnesses, infections, inappropriate clothing, aggression, and cruelty to others.

Emotional abuse is a pattern of behavior that attacks a child's emotional development and sense of self-worth. The warning signs are delayed physical, cognitive, and emotional development, wetting of pants or bed, sleep disturbances, ulcers, poor physical appearance, habit disorders, inappropriate aggression, poor peer relations, bizarre or self-destructive acts, extreme need for perfection, emotional extremes, nightmares, clinging, fear of adults, tics, phobias, obsessions, depression, low self-esteem or confidence, and family and peer conflicts.

School violence is unacceptable yet it happens every single day in America. Why has violence become such a part of our culture? Violence is now tolerated in most communities and schools. We talk about regaining the power to provide safe schools, yet we have bullying statistics that are out of proportion, attacks on teachers are up, students are being caught for having weapons at school, and children and youth are using violence as a way to solve problems or communicate their frustration with the existing school system.

- In a nationwide survey of high school students, about 6 percent reported not going to school on one or more days in the thirty days preceding the survey because they felt unsafe, either at school or on their way to and from school (CDC, 2012).

- Nearly 700,000 young people ages ten to twenty-four are treated in emergency departments each year, for injuries sustained due to violence-related assaults (CDC, 2012).
- On average, sixteen persons between the ages of ten and twenty-four are murdered each day in the United States (CDC, 2012).
- In addition to causing injury and death, youth violence affects communities by increasing the cost of health care, reducing productivity, decreasing property values, and disrupting social services (Mercy et al., 2002).
- Juveniles accounted for 16 percent of all violent crime arrests and 26 percent of all property crime arrests in 2008 (Puzzanchera, 2009).
- In 2008, 1,280 juveniles were arrested for murder, 3,340 for forcible rape, and 56,000 for aggravated assault (Puzzanchera, 2009).

A number of factors can increase the risk of a youth engaging in violence, but the presence of these factors does not always mean that a young person will become an offender. Research associates the following risk factors with perpetration of youth violence (DHHS, 2001; Lipsey and Derzon, 1998; Resnick et al., 2004):

- Prior history of violence
- Drug, alcohol, or tobacco use
- Association with delinquent peers
- Poor family functioning
- Poor grades in school
- Poverty in the community

Individual Risk Factors

- History of violent victimization
- Attention deficits, hyperactivity, or learning disorders
- History of early aggressive behavior
- Involvement with drugs, alcohol, or tobacco
- Low IQ
- Poor behavioral control
- Deficits in social cognitive or information-processing abilities
- High emotional distress
- History of treatment for emotional problems
- Antisocial beliefs and attitudes
- Exposure to violence and conflict in the family

Family Risk Factors

- Authoritarian childrearing attitudes

- Harsh, lax, or inconsistent disciplinary practices
- Low parental involvement
- Low emotional attachment to parents or caregivers
- Low parental education and income
- Parental substance abuse or criminality
- Poor family functioning
- Poor monitoring and supervision of children

Peer/Social Risk Factors

- Association with delinquent peers
- Involvement in gangs
- Social rejection by peers
- Lack of involvement in conventional activities
- Poor academic performance
- Low commitment to school and school failure

Community Risk Factors

- Diminished economic opportunities
- High concentrations of poor residents
- High level of transiency
- High level of family disruption
- Low levels of community participation
- Socially disorganized neighborhood

This list is by no means exhaustive.

ONGOING STRATEGIES TO IMPROVE THE ISSUE—HOW CAN WE MAKE IT BETTER?

Protective Factors for the Perpetration of Youth Violence

Protective factors buffer young people from the risks of becoming violent. These factors exist at various levels. To date, protective factors have not been studied as extensively or rigorously as risk factors. However, identifying and understanding protective factors are equally as important as researching risk factors.

Studies propose the following protective factors (DHHS, 2001; Resnick et al., 2004):

Individual/Family Protective Factors

- Intolerant attitude toward deviance
- High IQ
- High grade point average
- Positive social orientation
- Religiosity
- Connectedness to family or adults outside the family
- Ability to discuss problems with parents
- Perceived parental expectations about school performance are high
- Frequent shared activities with parents
- Consistent presence of parent during at least one of the following: when awakening, when arriving home from school, at evening mealtime, or going to bed
- Involvement in social activities

Peer/Social Protective Factors

- Commitment to school
- Involvement in social activities

An observation of the at-risk factors and the protective factors helps us see very easily that there are more at-risk factors present that will lead to the likeliness of a youth acting out. However the list for protective factors is much less comprehensive, but is very much based on relationships with others. The power of people cannot be underestimated—adults can be a positive factor in prevention.

Weapons in the school and community are ever present—the key is to be able to identify whether or not the person has a weapon and whether their behavior indicates that they may use it. Michael and Chris Dorn produced a checklist of seven indicators that a weapon is being concealed. It is a well-known fact that an aggressor can belong to any race or ethnic group. They can be from a variety of socio-economic groups and may have a PH.D or be a high school dropout. It can be anyone.

Learn to Recognize These Behaviors: Officers and other campus person-nel, such as school counselors and faculty members, have learned to identify the specific indicators that a person may be armed. Below are a few of the most common. It should be noted, however, that the following signs do not always indicate the presence of a weapon:

1. Security Check: Gun violators in particular will typically touch and/or adjust the weapons concealed on their bodies numerous times during the day. This may be a gentle and difficult to observe bump with the

elbow, wrist, or hand. On rare occasions, it could be a distinct grasping of the weapon as they adjust it. Violators often make this gesture when getting out of a chair or a car or when walking up a flight of stairs or high curb.

2. Unnatural Gait: Gun violators may walk with an awkward gait. They may fail to bend their knees because they have rifles or shotguns in their pants. They may also walk uncomfortably because they have guns, knives or other weapons hidden in their boots or shoes causing discomfort. Again, the total circumstances will indicate the likelihood of a weapon being present.

   For example, an individual with a disability may also not bend the leg or walk with an unnatural gait, but he or she will likely not appear to be nervous. You will also not see the rigid line of a rifle running down the outer pants leg as the person walks or the periodic bulge from the butt of the gun above the waistband as it moves back and forth.

3. Jacket Sag: When you place a handgun in a jacket pocket, the coat typically hangs lower on the side where the weapon is located. In addition, you will often see the fabric pulled tight from the weight of the gun, and the weapon may swing as a violator walks. Often, the outline of the weapon may be observed in the pocket area. In some cases, the violator will attempt to hold or pin the weapon, if it begins to swing or beat against their body.

   In cases where the violator becomes extremely nervous when approached by an officer, he or she may actually grasp the weapon to keep it from swinging or put a hand in the pocket. While this is often seen when people have items other than a weapon in their pocket, it is also an indicator that is very typical of the gun violator, particularly when observed with other behaviors described here.

4. Hunchback Stride: When trying to conceal a shotgun, rifle, or submachine gun under a coat while walking, the butt of the weapon will often cause a noticeable bulge behind the armpit. Additionally, the jacket does not move naturally because it is supported by the outline of the weapon. Also, when someone wears a shoulder holster or straps on a sawed-off rifle, shotgun, or submachine gun under his or her arm, a bulge in front of or behind the armpit will often be visible.

5. Bulges and the Outline of a Weapon: An alert officer can often spot the telltale bulge of the weapon or, in some instances, the distinct outline of a handgun, knife, or brass knuckles in a violator's pocket. This may also sometimes be observed in a woman's purse, book bag, or other hand-carried item. In some instances, violators wrap a long gun in a blanket or long jacket.

6. Visible Weapon: Clearly the most reliable of all the indicators is when the weapon can actually be seen. It is astounding how many times an armed intruder has entered a facility with a rifle or shotgun protruding from under his or her jacket, without being observed by staff. In some cases, the butt of a handgun is visible because it is sticking out from a back or front pocket. A more common instance is the clip-on pocket-knife that can be observed clipped to a front pocket or in the waist-band.

7. Palming: Most often observed with the edged weapon violator but occasionally seen with gun violators, palming behaviors often indicate imminent risk to the observer. The knife violator may run the blade of the weapon up along the arm or behind the leg to conceal it from frontal view. Just before a target is attacked, a violator will also typically have his or her eyes fixed on the intended victim (Dorn, 2006).

WHAT CAN YOU DO NOW?

Research shows that the following characteristics are common among schools that are effective in building and maintaining a positive school climate, as well as in preventing school violence:

1. Positive relationship-building. Intentional efforts are made to build and maintain caring and supportive relationships among students, teachers, and other school staff members, and families.
2. Sense of belonging. In addition to positive relationships, both students and staff experience school as meaningful, productive, and relevant. Active student participation in decision making is emphasized, as well as activities, such as service learning, that promote a sense of community and belonging.
3. Positive behavior supports. Emphasis is placed on the use of positive rather than punitive techniques.
4. High expectations. Teachers, students, and parents expect success in both academic and behavioral endeavors and provide the necessary supports to achieve these expectations.
5. Social and emotional skills. Deliberate efforts are made to develop social and emotional competencies among all students.
6. Parent and community involvement. Family and community members are viewed as valuable resources and their active involvement in the school's mission is strongly encouraged.
7. Fairness and clarity of rules. Students perceive rules as being clear, fair, and not overly harsh.

8. School safety. Students, teachers, and families perceive the school as safe (Consortium to Prevent School Violence, 2010).

TIPS FOR TEACHERS

Abuse

Once a report has been made to the Child Protection Agency (CPA), several procedures are followed. The CPA begins to collect the following information to assess the situation:

- summary of suspected abuse and neglect (who, what, where, when, number of incidents, degree of current risk, medical attention, presence of domestic violence)
- the child (who, where, whom the child is with, school, grade, home address, child's relationship to offender, any disabilities, who is available for support)
- the alleged abuser/person (name, where he or she is now, place of employment, home address, current relationship with child, access to child, history of violence, mental health, criminal behavior, awareness of the referral)
- non-offending parent (who, place of employment, contact information, current relationship to offender, any knowledge of abuse, does this person possess the ability to protect the child, extended family or support groups)
- siblings or other children in the home (names, schools, current whereabouts, other siblings being abused or who know of abuse)
- other household members (names, ages, genders, relationships, involvement in or knowledge of alleged abuse)
- referral source (name, relationship to the family, how the source knows about the abuse, whether he or she has directly observed the abuse or knows how the family will react to the assessment, why the referral is made now, any other individuals who know about the abuse, any other insights about the family)

If a child discloses abuse, it is important that the educator remain calm and supportive. If the disclosure occurs during instruction, it is important that the educator acknowledge the disclosure but maintain strict confidentiality in the discussion and action of the disclosure. If teachers suspect abuse, they should not pressure the child to disclose but simply report what they have observed.

Teachers should remember the following guidelines when dealing with abuse:

- Follow your school's protocol for reporting.
- Remain calm, keep an open mind, and do not make judgments.

- Support the child with active listening.
- Find a quiet place to talk to the child.
- Reassure the child that he or she has done the right thing by telling someone.
- Listen to the child without interruptions. Let him or her talk openly about the situation and record concrete information.
- Tell the child that there is help available.
- Reassure the child that you will do your best to protect and support him or her.
- Let the child know you must report the abuse to someone who has helped other children like him or her and their families.
- Report the incident to the proper authorities.
- Let the child know what will happen when the report is made, if you have the appropriate information.
- Seek out your own support persons to help you work through your feelings about the disclosure, if needed.
- Be aware of personal issues and how they affect your perception.
- Do not promise confidentiality.
- Remember that you are not responsible for investigating the claims, only reporting. Child Protective Services will do the investigations (State of New Hampshire, 2002).

Individual teachers are in a unique situation to recognize and report suspected cases of child abuse and neglect. Effective prevention programs reduce the number of victims, while educating a broader cross section of the public. Schools can become advocates for abuse-prevention education and student assistance. Programs and curricula that give children an understanding of appropriate and inappropriate behaviors, that incorporate information on sex and sexual health, and that share resources such as access to clinics and support groups are useful in the prevention of child abuse and neglect. As educators and parents, we can get children the mental health help they need to develop healthy developing brains and minds that feel safe and develop impulse control to prevent aggression and violence.

REFERENCES

American Psychological Association (APA). (2003). Protecting our children from abuse and neglect. Washington, DC: APA.

Boseley, S. (2013, September 18). High gun ownership makes countries less safe, US study finds. *The Guardian*. Retrieved October 10, 2013, from http://www.theguardian.com/world/2013/sep/18/gun-ownership-gun-deaths-study.

Centers for Disease Control and Prevention. Web-based Injury Statistics Query and Reporting System (WISQARS) [Online]. (2012) National Center for Injury Prevention and Control, Centers for Disease Control and Prevention (producer). Available from http://www.cdc.gov/injury/wisqars/index.html.

Consortium to Prevent School violence, Bullying Prevention Fact Sheet. Retrieved June 2, 2013, from www. preventschoolviolence.org/resources.html.

Department of Health and Human Services (DHHS). Youth violence: a report of the Surgeon General [online]; 2001. Available from www.surgeongeneral.gov/library/youthviolence/toc.html.

Department of Health and Human Services (DHHS). Youth violence: a report of the Surgeon General [online]; 2001. Available from www.surgeongeneral.gov/library/youthviolence/toc.html, http://www.apa.org/monitor/julaug04/stopping.aspx.

Dorn, M., Dorn, C. (2006, July/August). Seven signs a weapon is being concealed. Campus Safety Magazine.

Lipsey, M. W., Derzon, J. H. (1998). Predictors of violent and serious delinquency in adolescence and early adulthood: a synthesis of longitudinal research. In: Loeber R., Farrington D. P., editors. Serious and violent juvenile offenders: risk factors and successful interventions. Thousand Oaks (CA): Sage Publications; 86–105.

Mercy, J., Butchart, A., Farrington, D., Cerdá, M. Youth violence. In Krug, E., Dahlberg, L. L., Mercy, J. A., Zwi, A. B., Lozano, R., editors. World report on violence and health. Geneva (Switzerland): World Health Organization; 2002. pp. 25–56.

Perry, B. (n.d.). Aggression and Violence: The Neurobiology of Experience. *Scholastic, Helping Children Around the World to Read and Learn. Scholastic.com.* Retrieved October 11, 2013 from http://teacher.scholastic.com/professional/ bruceperry/aggression_violence.htm.

Puzzanchera, C. (2009). Juvenile Arrests 2008. Washington, DC: U.S. Department of Justice, Office of Justice Programs, Office of Juvenile Justice and Delinquency Prevention.

Resnick, M. D., Ireland, M., Borowsky, I. (2004). Youth violence perpetration: what protects? What predicts? Findings from the National Longitudinal Study of Adolescent Health. Journal of Adolescent Health, 35(424), 1–10.

State of New Hampshire, Office of the Attorney General, Task Force on Child Abuse and Neglect. 2002. Child abuse and neglect: Guidelines for New Hampshire school employees: Recognizing and reporting suspected child abuse and neglect. 2nd ed. Concord, NH: Department of Education.

Part III

Strategies for Building a Healthy Brain and Mind

Chapter Eleven

Mindfulness, Meditation, and Sleep

One of the best strategies we can teach our children to improve their brains and minds as well as their safety, happiness, mental health, and overall healthy development is the art of mindfulness. One strategy that can improve mindfulness is meditation, but mindfulness goes beyond just purposeful meditation. This chapter will discuss the importance of mindfulness and how to teach meditation and encourage its regular practice among children. In addition, this chapter will discuss the importance of sleep. This topic is included here because like with meditation, the brain is still active, but quieted during sleep, and sleep is so important for brain and mind health.

The question is—how do mindfulness, meditation, and sleep help children in their development? How important are they? How might building more mindfulness and meditation into a child's life help their developing brains and minds? How can we create healthy sleep patterns for children?

NATURE OF THE ISSUE AND HOW IT AFFECTS CHILDREN

When children are young, they naturally function "in the moment." They tend not to focus on the past (partly because they do not have much of a past) or the future (perhaps because their abstract thinking, language, and executive functioning centers are not as well developed). It is not until these areas of the brain become well-developed that our minds pull us out of the present moment and focus our attention on the running language-laden monolog in our heads. This voice pulls us into thinking about the past or the future— neither of which we can change or control. We often dwell on the past or worry about the future—but we can do nothing to change the past and we cannot predict the future.

Mindfulness is paying close attention to what is happening and what one is experiencing in the present moment—taking time to focus on what one is doing, eating, reading, saying, hearing, and so on. In mindfulness we are fully present in the present moment. The present moment is where we live and exist, yet our older adult (and even older child) brains are rarely focused there. When in the present moment, children can be naturally more mindful. A keen attention to the present is an essential part of mindfulness that can contribute to success in school and at home or on the playground or playing field. Children who are more mindful have an easier time in these spaces.

Flow is a concept that has been described and written extensively about by Mihály Csíkszentmihályi. When in a state of "flow" we are completely single-minded in focus with our positive energy focused on a particular task or experience. People experience a sense of joy and peace when in this state. Athletes discuss being in a state of flow when they lose track of time and are singularly focused on the sport they are playing. They are fully present in the moment without any distractions of anxieties or worries. People sometimes call this experience in athletics as "being in the zone." But the truth is, this experience can happen reading a book, doing a school project, giving a talk, eating a great meal, spending time with friends, meditating, etc.

For flow to be achieved Csíkszentmihályi argues that there are generally two conditions:

1. involvement in an activity with clearly set goals and progress and structure
2. those doing the task receive clear and immediate feedback about their performance. This helps create a good balance between one's perception of his/her skills/abilities and the task at hand—one must have confidence about his/her abilities (Csikszentmihalyi, Abuhamdeh, & Nakamura, 2005).

We can create opportunities for children to experience flow in their lives by helping them balance their abilities, and confidence levels with activities they enjoy, are good at and for which they can get immediate feedback to improve their skills and performance. We hope that students can have these kinds of experiences in school and in school-related activities. And if they cannot experience flow in school, we hope that parents can find ways to help them achieve their flow experience in healthy ways through arts/music/dance or other experiences outside.

As Daniel Willingham (2009) argues in his book, *Why Don't Students Like School?* "contrary to popular belief, the brain is not designed for thinking. It's designed to save you from having to think, because the brain is actually not very good at thinking" (p. 3). As we teach children to become more mindful, they can become more purposeful in their thinking—that is, they can become better able to direct and control their thinking.

The notion of mindfulness is the idea that we focus on our experience of reality as it exists in the present moment. That we pay close attention to our experiences and what is going on around us. We become keen observers of our emotional states and what our minds are doing. If you watch a very young child, he or she will tend to be very focused on what is going on at the present moment. This is why they will often ask questions about what is happening to them or what they notice: "I'm hungry" or "What makes the car go?" or "Why do dogs pant?" or "This ice cream is delicious."

When they start to get older and more aware of past and future and their role in it, they start to focus more on what happened in the past or what might happen in the future. Children may start to become upset about events in the past or anxious or worried or excited about the future.

As adults we are guilty of this past and future focus too. Our brains are so busy thinking about what has happened or what might happen that they are seldom focused on what is currently happening. We all know those times when we are in a "zone" and so focused on the present moment (usually doing what we love, or times of high emotion, or intense pain).

As children age, we spend so much time encouraging them to focus on the future. With all this time focused on the past and future, it is no wonder that as children get older, they have greater difficulty paying full attention to what is happening now. If children are not paying full attention to what they are doing in the moment, they are at greater risk of accidents. They are also more likely to have difficulty paying attention to what is happening (or what they are supposed to be learning) in the classroom.

They have greater difficulty controlling their emotions and making good decisions. They may have sleep difficulties as well because they cannot shut their brains down enough to sleep. A tired mind has great difficulty focusing on the present moment. It is easily distracted. Sleep is essential for the brain and mind to function properly.

THE VITAL IMPORTANCE OF SLEEP FOR HEALTHY BRAIN AND MIND DEVELOPMENT

We have not devoted an entire chapter to the importance of sleep and rest for healthy brain and mind development, but it is so vitally important that perhaps we should have. We included sleep with mindfulness because mindfulness and controlling one's mind can likely help with healthy sleep patterns—and healthy sleep patterns make mindfulness easier as the brain and mind do not function well when tired.

The truth is that consistently researchers have shown that sleep is critical in the consolidation of new memories and that the number of REM (Rapid Eye Movement) cycles each night is important to making sure that key memories are created. As children are in school each day and learning new things, sleep becomes essential for memories to be created and retained.

According to the researchers at the department of Sleep Medicine at Harvard Medical School, there are three major stages of memory formation, and sleep researchers have shown that sleep affects each of these, although the exact mechanisms are still being examined:

> "Acquisition refers to the introduction of new information into the brain. Consolidation represents the processes by which a memory becomes stable. Recall refers to the ability to access the information (whether consciously or unconsciously) after it has been stored" (Sleep, Learning and Memory, 2007).

Children tend not to get sufficient sleep. Part of the difficulty of sleep is simply lack of time for sleep—they are busy in sports, schoolwork, or other activities (television, video gaming, etc.) so they do not get to bed early enough and get up early for school. Most bedtimes for young children are not early enough. Adolescents need a great deal of sleep and are much less likely to get sufficient sleep. "Restricted sleep" in adolescents is defined as six hours or less per night and in a 2010 study researchers showed that as high as 20 percent of children between eleven and seventeen consistently had restricted sleep and 54 percent had multiple extended periods of restricted sleep that impacted performance (Roberts, Roberts, and Xing, 2011).

Children and adolescents need more sleep than you/they think to learn well. A recent study published in the *Journal of Epidemiology and Community Health* included over 11,000 child participants at the ages of three, five, and seven. Researchers found that youngsters who went to bed at irregular hours scored lower in cognitive tests for reading, math, and spatial abilities. Those who went to sleep at roughly the same time every night received better scores on math and reading skills. The researchers noted brain plasticity (the brain's ability to learn, change, develop) is affected by sleep (Kelly, Kelly, & Sacker, 2012).

This study also supported the notion that insufficient sleep has effects that are cumulative and has different effects depending on gender. For example, the authors suggest that girls who had "never" gone to bed at a consistent bedtime showed significantly lower scores in all cognitive areas tested. They also scored lower if they only had irregular bedtime hours at the age of seven. Age matters too. Girls who had irregular bedtimes only at the age of five showed lower reading scores and boys at that age showed lower math scores. In addition, both groups with irregular sleep showed social problems at school as well.

Sleep is critical for good cognitive functioning. As John Medina (n.d.) supports from his review of the research on sleep and learning:

- "When we're asleep, the brain is not resting at all. It is almost unbelievably active! It's possible that the reason we need to sleep is so that we can learn.
- Sleep must be important because we spend 1/3 of our lives doing it! Loss of sleep hurts attention, executive function, working memory, mood, quantitative skills, logical reasoning, and even motor dexterity.
- We still don't know how much we need! It changes with age, gender, pregnancy, puberty, and so much more.
- Napping is normal. Ever feel tired in the afternoon? That's because your brain really wants to take a nap. There's a battle raging in your head between two armies. Each army is made of legions of brain cells and biochemicals—one desperately trying to keep you awake, the other desperately trying to force you to sleep. Around 3 p.m., 12 hours after the midpoint of your sleep, all your brain wants to do is nap.
- Taking a nap might make you more productive. In one study, a 26-minute nap improved NASA pilots' performance by 34 percent.
- Don't schedule important meetings at 3 p.m. It just doesn't make sense."

To be able to sleep well, it helps often to be able to slow down and control our thinking or become more mindful and able to let go of thinking that can become obsessive or harmful. Letting go of thoughts that are recurrent and serving no purpose except to upset us is important within mindfulness—as we become more aware of what our minds are doing, then we become better able to let things go. Perhaps this will help with healthy sleep as well.

ONGOING STRATEGIES TO IMPROVE THE ISSUE — HOW CAN WE MAKE THIS BETTER?

Meditation

Many different forms of meditation exist from guided meditation to Zen meditation, Yoga meditation, walking meditation, mindfulness meditation, and so on.... World famous Deepak Chopra defines meditation on his website in this very powerful and elegantly simple quote:

> "Meditation is a tool for the re-discovery of the body's own inner intelligence. Practiced for thousands of years, it's not about forcing the mind to be quiet; it's finding the silence that's already there and making it a part of your life. From this field of pure potentiality we get our bursts of inspiration, our most

intuitive thoughts, and our deepest sense of connection to the universe" (Chopra, 2013).

The benefits of meditation are many from helping with anxiety to reducing aggression and fear to greater self-control, fewer accidents, improved health, and greater life satisfaction. The act of slowing down one's mind and focusing on one's breathing rather than racing thoughts or distractions or triggers for problematic behaviors can go a long way toward helping children learn to control their minds rather than being controlled by their minds. There are resources available for children to teach more guided meditation, and in this digital age, perhaps to get children started, downloading a good guided meditation application or audio or visual might be helpful.

Meditation can be as simple as focusing on one's breath in and out. Explain to children that they can try to allow all their attention to be on their breath as it goes in and goes out. They can count breaths or have a syllable or sound that accompanies the breath ("in"/ "out"). They can picture where the breath goes throughout the body as it goes in. Encourage them to feel their body relax as they do this and feel the parts of their body relax as they continue to slow their breathing and heart rate. Explain that as other thoughts come in they can picture them just floating in and floating out and to try not to grab onto a thought as it floats in.

Swami Rama in his discussion of teaching traditional meditation of the Himilayan Masters to children states that meditation allows us to become more in touch with ourselves and our thinking—in particular our inner monolog. He suggests we need to learn to discriminate what we select and reject to listen to and develop and how to work with ourselves and our minds:

> As a part of our educational training we must define spirituality in its most precise and universal terms. Spirituality means that which helps us to discipline our thoughts, speech, and actions; that which leads us toward the center of consciousness, and thereby helps to unfold our inner potentials. Education based on such spiritual guidelines will help humanity to become self-reliant and confident. Only education based on spirituality can bring harmonious balance to both our external and inner life (From Swami Rama's *Let the Bud of Life Bloom: A Guide to Raising Happy and Healthy Children*).

We need to provide our children time and space to be with the quiet of their minds—without racing around from task to task or without the space being filled by electronic devices and ways to shut the mind off completely.

TIME FOR CALM AND REST

So many children are so busy throughout the day. And even those who aren't occupy their minds with television or other video screens that are in constant motion. Children (and adults too) need time for calm and quiet throughout the day. It is time to let the brain be quiet. Although we have a difficult time stopping the incessant stream of thoughts in our brains, taking time for meditation will help with that and offer that space for quiet and ceasing the endless stream of thoughts about past and future that can overwhelm us and our children.

Sufficient Sleep

The brain is always active, particularly during sleep. Sleep is essential for learning. John Medina wrote in his overview of research on the brain that "loss of sleep hurts attention, executive function, working memory, mood, quantitative skills, logical reasoning, and even motor dexterity" (Medina, 2008, para. 2). While it is unclear exactly how much sleep is needed, as it appears to be affected by age, fitness, puberty, gender, and so on, we need enough to have a sufficient number of REM cycles. There is some evidence supporting naps and explains why so many of us are tired around 3 pm. As Medina wrote, "Around 3 pm, 12 hours after the midpoint of your sleep, all your brain wants to do is nap . . . don't schedule important meetings at 3 pm. It just doesn't make sense." He, like so many others, advocates napping around this time instead.

How Much Sleep Do Children and Adolescents Need?

There isn't complete agreement on exactly how much sleep each individual person needs— this can be variable, but the National Sleep Foundation makes some good recommendations for each age group:

- Newborn babies—twelve to eighteen hours of sleep
- 1 to 3-year-olds—twelve to fourteen hours of sleep
- Preschoolers—eleven to thirteen hours of sleep
- 5 to 10-year-olds—ten to eleven hours of sleep
- Teenagers—8.5 to 9.25 hours of sleep

Routines at bedtime are key, and remaining consistent in the enforcement of these routines.

- Turn off electronic devices—such as video games, computers, and television about a half hour before the set bedtime. Television and games can make sleep difficult.
- Also it is a good idea to keep video games, computers, and televisions out of young persons' bedrooms.

- Avoid all caffeine including sodas, teas, coffee, drinks or chocolate. These are not healthy and have other problems as well, but cutting them out entirely will help sleep.
- Create a good sleeping space—make sure the room is dark, cool, and has no distractions.
- Bedtime stories, lullabies, baths, and reading are good rituals for younger children. As children become independent readers, encourage them to continue reading or having their own quiet time before bed. (You may need to take away cell phones at a certain time to avoid middle of the night texting, etc.)

WHAT CAN YOU DO RIGHT NOW?

FOCUS ON NOW: As Eckhart Tolle (1999) wrote in his book, *The Power of Now: A Guide to Spiritual Enlightenment,* "Realize deeply that the present moment is all you have. Make the NOW the primary focus of your life." He elaborates further: "Time isn't precious at all, because it is an illusion. What you perceive as precious is not time but the one point that is out of time: the Now. That is precious indeed. The more you are focused on time —past and future—the more you miss the Now, the most precious thing there is."

1. Redirect children's attention to the moment—help them see what is important to attend to and why.
2. Redirect your own attention to the present moment.
3. Take time out yourself for meditation or breathing (model it for children).
4. Encourage children to focus on their breathing throughout the day (give regular reminders).
5. Practice meditation—use guided meditation resources (recordings, etc.) if helpful, and encourage children to take time to meditate at regular periods each day.
6. Make sure to leave enough time in the day for sleep and consider naptime for children and adults alike.

Rudy Tanzi (2013) in his PBS series "Super Brain" proposes a method called STOP that people can use when they are upset or something sudden and troubling or difficult happens:

- Stop
- Take three deep breaths
- Observe how you feel
- Proceed with awareness and compassion

These are just some selected strategies to enhance mindfulness, meditation, and sleep for children and for you as educator/parent to be able to be more effective and present in your engagement with children and their growth and development.

TIPS FOR TEACHERS

1. Teach, encourage, and model mindfulness for students—that is, focusing deeply on this moment and what is happening and our connection within it and to it.
2. Teach children how to meditate and the importance of slowing one's mind down and focusing on breathing and calming down.
3. Make sure students are getting sufficient sleep—if they are not, find out why and work with students to try to figure out how to help them structure their time so that they receive sufficient sleep.

REFERENCES

Chopra, Deepak. "Meditation, The Chopra Center." Meditation, The Chopra Center. N.p., n.d. Web. Accessed June 5, 2013.

Csikszentmihalyi, M., Abuhamdeh, S., & Nakamura, J. (2005), "Flow," in Elliot, A. *Handbook of Competence and Motivation*, New York: The Guilford Press, pp. 598–698.

Kelly, Y., Kelly, J., & Sacker, A. (2012, October 4). Time for bed: associations with cognitive performance in 7-year-old children: a longitudinal population-based study—Kelly et al. Journal of Epidemiology & Community Health. Journal of Epidemiology & Community Health BMJ Journals. Retrieved August 22, 2013, from http://jech.bmj.com/content/early/2013/07/11/jech-2012-202024.full.

Medina, J. (2008). Brain Rules: 12 Principles for Surviving and Thriving at Work, Home and School. Pear Press, Seattle, WA.

Medina, J. (n.d.). Rule number 7: Sleep well, think well. Retrieved October 13, 2013, fromhttp://www.brainrules.net/sleep.

Rama, S. (2002). *Let the bud of life bloom: a guide to raising happy a nd healthy children*. Dehradun, India: Himalayan Institute Hospital Trust.

Roberts, R. E., Roberts, C., and Xing, Y. (2011). Restricted Sleep Among Adolescents: Prevalence, Incidence, Persistence, and Associated Factors. Behavioral Sleep Medicine, 9(1). Retrieved May 28, 2013, from http://www.tandfonline.com/doi/abs/10.108.

Sleep, Learning, and Memory. Healthy Sleep. (2007, December 18). Healthy Sleep. Retrieved May 22, 2013, from http://healthysleep.med.harvard.edu/healthy/matters/benefits-of-sleep/learningmemory.

Tanzi, Rudy. "Super Brain." Super Brain. PBS. 4 June, 2013. Television.

Tolle, Eckhart. The Power of Now: A Guide to Spiritual Enlightenment. Novato, CA: New World Library, 1999.

Willingham, D. T. (2009). Why Don't Students Like School? A Cognitive Scientist Answers Questions about how the Mind Works and What It Means for the Classroom. John Wiley and Sons: San Francisco, CA.

Chapter Twelve

Purposeful Teaching of Thinking/ Cognition and Identifying and Building Cognitive Strengths

If, as Willingham (2009) suggests in the previous chapter, our brains try to avoid purposeful or challenging thinking and are in fact designed to prevent us from thinking or at least try to streamline our thinking as much as possible, what do we as teachers and leaders need to do to help our students and ultimately our society learn to develop skills they need to become more purposeful critical thinkers and problem solvers? How might we know if a child has a problem with thinking that requires special attention?

Willingham (2009) suggests that "people are naturally curious, but we are not naturally good thinkers; unless the cognitive conditions are right, we will avoid thinking . . . by thinking I mean solving problems, reasoning, reading something complex or doing any mental work that requires some effort." Because of this he argues that "in order to maximize the likelihood that students will get the pleasurable rush that comes from successful thought . . . [we need to have students] working on problems that are of the right level of difficulty [because this] is rewarding, but working on problems that are too easy or too difficult is unpleasant." We need to find a balance between challenging mental work that is not too difficult and not too easy.

This is challenging in a classroom of twenty-plus different learners with different ability levels, but it can be done, and it is easier when parents are also working with their children at their individual levels of ability. We need to figure out what each child's abilities are in different areas and construct instruction that is challenging, but can still allow the child to be successful. With computer-aided instruction, programs can tailor assessments to students' abilities. We can and should be able to determine instructional needs based on these abilities as well.

NATURE OF THE ISSUE AND HOW IT AFFECTS CHILDREN

Children in the United States spend a great many of their waking hours in some kind of structured education—most spend this time in schools. However, a child's learning is not limited to the school building. A child's brain is always learning, growing, developing, and maturing—reaching full maturity and development around age twenty-five. Adult care providers and teachers alike should have a basic understanding about how the brain works to facilitate the best possible learning environment for young people.

Knowing how the brain learns will help parents and teachers alike in creating this best possible environment both at home and in schools. Success in school can provide resiliency for even the most at-risk child. Helping children become excited about learning and how their own brains learn can be a powerful strategy for promoting their emotional and physical well-being.

General Background on How the Brain Learns

With the advent of functional magnetic resonance imaging (fMRI) to examine the brain in action, research in cognitive neuroscience has provided wonderful new insight into how the brain learns. Substantial work still needs to be done in this area to be able to make sweeping proposals for change in schools and learning at home, but there are some major ideas and themes that parents, teachers, and others working with children can use to improve learning for all children.

As teachers and leaders, we need to model good and purposeful critical thinking and problem solving for our students. Then we must intentionally teach students thinking skills and ways to represent their thinking in specific ways. And finally, we need to assess student thinking as part of our assessment of student learning because in education "what gets tested/assessed is what gets taught." We also need to enhance motivation and persistence in the face of academic challenges. Children who learn to give up in the face of a challenge will have difficulty throughout their lifetime.

What Have We Learned about the Brain and Learning?

Early cognitive scientists and philosophers examined cognition decades and even centuries ago and the struggle to understand the brain, mind, and thinking continues unabated today. We have made great strides in understanding the brain and mind over the past couple of decades. As a result of the work of cognitive psychologists, neuroscientists, educators, and other researchers, there are some ways we can think about and teach thinking in more purposeful ways.

We have a greater understanding that new learning is connected to prior knowledge. We all build new learning on what we already know. As a parent, teacher, or other person working with children, it is critical that you try to connect new material with what a child already knows. We want to build a child's knowledge base so s/he has more prior knowledge to connect to new information. We need to encourage learning of factual knowledge early and ideally through reading and engagement with others—not from television (reasons will be described later in the chapter).

We also know that emotions are critical to learning and memory. We remember best what we care most about or have strong emotional associations with or think most about. We remember traumatic events vividly because of the strong emotional connection and because we think about them a lot. Teachers, parents, and others concerned with children's learning need to help children make meaningful connections about what they are learning. Long-term stress and trauma can inhibit classroom learning. But positive emotional associations can facilitate learning. As teachers and parents (acting as a child's at-home teacher), we must pay attention to a learning child's emotional state.

We know that children need opportunities for rehearsal/practice/feedback when they are learning new information. Children need opportunities to practice skills and concepts that they have learned, and they need to do this with adults who can give them thoughtful, useful, and immediate feedback on their understanding and performance. Real learning is transferred from the classroom to a child's world outside. Families and schools working together have the best chance of learning success if they work to facilitate this kind of transfer of learning from the classroom to the world outside.

We need to teach kids that intelligence is multifaceted and dynamic. Researchers have found that children who believe that intelligence can be changed often work harder on challenging tasks than those children who believe that intelligence is fixed. We need to praise students for their efforts in overcoming such academic challenges rather than on their intelligence (or our perceptions of their intelligence). Thus, it is better to say to a child, "I really like how hard you worked on that assignment . . . or wow, that hard work really paid off" than "wow, you're really smart—or you must be smart like your sister."

When we attribute our success to our own innate intelligence, we become more invested in not making any mistakes, lest someone find out we are not actually that "smart." (This is if we believe intelligence to be a fixed trait.) However, if we believe that we can work hard and get smarter and do better, then we are much less afraid of making mistakes or failing—we try harder because we know that hard work can and will pay off eventually. Intelligence can increase with environmental and academic inputs that are conducive. Also, Howard Gardner proposes in his book *Frames of Mind* (2006) that there is not a single "intelligence" but rather "multiple intelligences" (described later in this chapter).

We know that the brain sequences information. We categorize information. We describe information. We know that we do have common ways of thinking or "cognitive universals," but a cohesive paradigm that is useful for teaching children in schools has been lacking. However, David Hyerle identified such a cohesive framework and "language for learning" showing the integration of eight universal forms of thinking and their graphic representations in the Thinking Maps® model (Hyerle, 2009). These eight cognitive universals are described in the next section. Teaching these eight forms of thinking, and helping children recognize when they are using them can be incredibly useful in getting children to become more purposeful thinkers.

To be able to think purposefully, we know that children's basic physical and psychological needs must be met. In addition, they must have opportunities to do cognitive work that engages them at multiple levels, and is challenging, but not beyond their ability. They need opportunities for success. They also must grapple with meaningful problems and questions that build upon a knowledge base that they must build. We need to ask good questions and allow students to engage in meaningful problem solving. In our ever-growing standardized educational world, these kinds of opportunities are becoming increasingly rare—particularly for our most academically at-risk children.

ONGOING STRATEGIES TO IMPROVE THE ISSUE—HOW CAN WE MAKE THIS BETTER?

As teachers and administrators are preparing students for the twenty-first century, and jobs and careers that don't exist yet, we must focus our instructional efforts explicitly on teaching children a grounding of knowledge, provide opportunities to build good habits of purposeful and critical thinking and support them as they engage in meaningful problem solving.

All thinking happens in the brain. The brain is a pattern detector: it is designed to process patterns of incoming information via the five senses—visual, auditory, tactile/touch, smell, and taste. But the brain does not experience these experiences directly as it sits in a dark box. It relies on electrical impulses that are stimulated by these experiences of seeing, hearing, tasting, smelling, and touching. These electrical patterns of firing that result in the brain create patterns and algorithms that the brain uses to interpret the patterns of information coming in from the senses, Jeff Hawkins argues, are the same for all senses (Hawkins, 2004).

The brain likes patterns. It creates patterns of neuronal firing. It is designed to make our lives easier and more efficient. The brain is designed to be efficient, so it tries to streamline our thinking as much as possible. This means the brain tends to like routines, but still enjoys a challenge—provided it can be successful. Successfully completing a challenging problem is very rewarding for the brain. It reinforces that behavior with pleasure chemicals in the brain (e.g., dopamine).

However, the brain does not like to fail or experience frustration. We all know that feeling of frustration and even anger when something is too difficult or challenging and we are not successful. Imagine as a student feeling this all the time. As parents and educators, the trick is to find the right balance between what is challenging and can allow students to be successful and what is too easy or boring or too difficult and frustrating (Willingham, 2009). This can be a fine line. However, finding it is crucial to the success of children's learning and their brains and minds continue to persevere.

Daniel Willingham offers "9-principles of the mind" that he grounds in research over the past few decades:

1. People are naturally curious, but we are not naturally good thinkers; unless the cognitive conditions are right, we will avoid thinking.
2. Factual knowledge must precede skill.
3. Memory is the residue of thought.
4. We understand new things in the context of things we already know, and most of what we know is concrete.
5. It is virtually impossible to become proficient at a mental task without extended practice.
6. Cognition early in training is fundamentally different from cognition late in training.
7. [People] are more alike than different in terms of how they think and learn.
8. [People] do differ in intelligence, but intelligence can be changed through sustained hard work.
9. Teaching, like any complex cognitive skill, must be practiced to be improved. (Quoted from Willingham, D. [2009] *Why Don't Students Like School?* Jossey Bass: San Francisco.)

Habits of Mind

In addition to these (and other) "principles of mind" proposed by Willingham, others have examined what kinds of "habits of mind" help students succeed in school and life. According to Art Costa and Bena Kallick, the creators of "Habits of Mind" there are sixteen "habits of mind" that are essential to success:

1. Persisting
2. Managing Impulsivity
3. Listening with Empathy and Understanding
4. Thinking Flexibly
5. Metacognition
6. Striving for Accuracy
7. Questioning and Posing Problems
8. Applying Past Knowledge to New Situations
9. Creating, Imagining, and Innovating
10. Finding Humor
11. Gathering Data Through All Senses
12. Remaining Open to Continuous Learning
13. Responding with Wonderment and Awe
14. Taking Responsible Risks
15. Thinking and Communicating with Clarity and Precision
16. Thinking Interdependently—From Institute for Habits of Mind (www.instituteforhabitsofmind.com)

As parents and teachers, we can encourage these habits of mind in children from a young age. Some of these habits are in the social/emotional realm and some are more focused on cognition. Cultivating successful thinking must incorporate both the social/emotional as well as the cognitive and more logical executive functioning.

Howard Gardner's Multiple Intelligence Theory

Howard Gardner offered a challenge to the common notions that intelligence is fixed and a single, measurable entity. His theory of Multiple Intelligences suggests that intelligence is more complex than the simple, singular notion of "general intelligence" that was measured by IQ tests. In this theory he posits eight intelligences and suggests that individuals have different profiles of strengths in each of these areas:

- Linguistic intelligence: A person who has linguistic intelligence is said to be very skilled with language and its usage. Poets and other writers or linguists have high linguistic intelligence.
- Logical-mathematical intelligence: A person with logical-mathematical intelligence has high ability in mathematics or with number systems and other complex logical systems.

- Musical intelligence: A person who is high in musical intelligence thinks in music or musically. He or she has the ability to understand and create music. Skilled musicians, composers, and dancers show a heightened musical intelligence.
- Spatial intelligence: People with spatial intelligence have the ability to recognize patterns and spatial relationships in the visual world. Artists, designers, and those who are able to think spatially are said to have high spatial intelligence.
- Bodily-kinesthetic intelligence: This entails the ability to use one's body well. Dancers and athletes are thought to have high bodily-kinesthetic intelligence.
- Interpersonal intelligence: People who are empathetic with others and can read and perceive other individuals' moods, desires, and motivations have high interpersonal intelligence.
- Intrapersonal intelligence: This entails having an understanding of one's own self.
- Later Gardner added an eighth intelligence, the naturalist intelligence, which entails the ability to work within nature and the natural world. Charles Darwin, he argues, possessed this form of intelligence.

Building on his work with multiple-intelligence theory, Gardner proposes the most essential kinds of "minds" we need to cultivate in ourselves and our young people in his book *Five Minds for the Future* (2007). The minds Gardner proposes are important for success not just in school but in adulthood in our ever-changing, technological, and global society. He proposes focusing on helping children (and adults) with developing the following:

- The disciplined mind: Young people need exposure to a variety of disciplines and a solid grounding in at least one discipline to be able to become very knowledgeable or even "expert" in their adulthood.
- The synthesizing mind: Children need to learn strategies for taking ideas and putting them together in ways that make sense for themselves and possibly improve understanding for others.
- The creative mind: We need to cultivate creativity in young people—to encourage children to think of unique ways of solving problems, to write their own songs, and to engage in the creation of new ideas and strategies. In Benjamin Bloom's revised taxonomy, the highest form of learning is believed to be creating new ideas or things.
- The respectful mind: As adults in our society, we must help children learn the skills of working and playing well with others. We need to teach children to respect, honor, and appreciate differences and provide opportunities for children to interact with others from diverse backgrounds.

- The ethical mind: Children learn a lot from watching adults. We need to model ethical behavior, especially in challenging situations. Discuss ethical dilemmas with children and talk about options for behavior in these complex situations. Talk with children about what it means to be a good citizen, a good worker, and a good person.

As adult caregivers and teachers, we need to think about the kinds of brains/minds we want to cultivate in our next generation—particularly to equip them with skills that will serve them well in the global marketplace of ideas and things. Gardner's framework provides us with some important points to consider when working with young people and their developing brains. For the theoretical framework from Howard Gardner and more information on the theory visit www.howardgardner.com.

As parents and teachers, we should pay attention to children's strengths in these areas. Schools have typically rewarded children with cognitive strengths in logical/mathematical intelligence and verbal/linguistic intelligence (and perhaps to a lesser degree visual/spatial intelligence). These are the abilities that get tested most often and where most instructional time is spent. Schools tend to consider musical/artistic intelligence to be more of a "talent" as is athletic ability (bodily-kinesthetic intelligence).

And those with social skills (or high interpersonal intelligences) may be rewarded in other ways (popularity, friends, teachers who like them), whereas those who are more quiet and contemplative (those with intrapersonal intelligence or those who are more existentialist) may be overlooked in school (unless they happen to also have strengths in the highly coveted verbal or mathematical realms. Truth is, we are not all equally good at all types of thinking. We have cognitive strengths.

As parents and teachers we can either build the strengths that children naturally seem to possess and cultivate those or we can continue to build strengths and nurture those areas that may not be as naturally strong. As parents and teachers we have our own strong suits in these areas too, so we need to recognize our own strengths or intelligences and work to develop others (which may be quite different from our own).

Motivation and Mindset

As Costa and Kallick describe persistence, "effacious people stick to a task until it is completed. They do not give up easily." However, the task must be believed to be achievable. As Daniel Pink in his book, *Drive*, notes, we are motivated by tasks that allow us a sense of autonomy, mastery, and purpose. Allowing students to have a sense of purpose in the work they are doing, particularly for complex learning tasks as well as giving them an opportunity to work independently to have a sense that they accomplished the task successfully (allowing a sense of mastery), will continue to motivate learners to persist in difficult situations.

In addition, Carol Dweck (2006) discusses the importance of having a "growth mindset" (believing that you can get smarter through hard work and persistence) versus a "fixed mindset" (believing that intelligence is fixed, so hard work will not make you smarter) will also help one persist in the face of challenging academic work. We reinforce the latter notion of intelligence as fixed (even though evidence suggests otherwise) every time we tell a child he or she is smart or not. Our comments and feedback to children should reflect their hard cognitive work rather than what we perceive to be their innate cognitive ability. So "that hard work really paid off on that test, didn't it?" is better than telling the child "great job—you're so smart!" The former promotes a growth mindset and promotes persistence and hard work in the face of cognitive challenges.

In addition there is the notion of "metacognition" or thinking about one's thinking. This ties in nicely with the previous chapter on mindfulness where one is observing what one is pondering in a given moment and learns to control and quiet the mind. As children become more aware of how they are thinking and what is influencing their thinking, then they can become more mindful, purposeful thinkers.

Asking Questions that Promote Problem Solving

Many people would likely argue that among the many outcomes we hope children get out of school is the ability to solve complex problems. In this age of information overload, the ability to manage a lot of information and use it to solve problems is ever-more crucial. There are many models of problem solving, but generally the steps of each tend to be consistently the following:

1. Identify the problem to be solved.
2. Analyze the nature and aspects/issues of the problem.
3. Brainstorm/identify potential solutions.
4. Select/weigh the best solutions.
5. Evaluate each selected solution.
6. Develop a plan of action.
7. Implement/act on the plan/solution.
8. Assess the effectiveness.

We want children to grow up to be able to be good problem-solvers and critical thinkers, yet we give them few opportunities to engage in these strategies. Willingham makes a compelling case that schools should be places where children learn "stuff" or key ideas, facts, and so on because without these basic building blocks of thought and problem solving and critical thinking, we can't do much creative thinking.

What Does It Mean to Be a Critical Thinker?

More than likely if we were all asked "should school engage students in critical thinking?" we would say "absolutely yes!" And yet, defining "critical thinking" is elusive. Many have attempted to define critical thinking and what is involved, but we have selected a definition from the Foundation for Critical Thinking that states that "a well cultivated critical thinker

*   raises vital questions and problems, formulating them clearly and precisely;
*   gathers and assesses relevant information, using abstract ideas to interpret it effectively, comes to well-reasoned conclusions and solutions, testing them against relevant criteria and standards;
*   thinks open-mindedly within alternative systems of thought, recognizing and assessing, as need be, their assumptions, implications, and practical consequences; and
*   communicates effectively with others in figuring out solutions to complex problems.

Critical thinking is, in short, self-directed, self-disciplined, self-monitored, and self-corrective thinking. It presupposes assent to rigorous standards of excellence and mindful command of their use. It entails effective communication and problem-solving abilities and a commitment to overcome our native egocentrism and sociocentrism. (Taken from Richard Paul and Linda Elder, The Miniature Guide to Critical Thinking Concepts and Tools, Foundation for Critical Thinking Press, 2008. Taken verbatim from www.criticalthinking.org.

Bloom's Taxonomy

In the field of education, Bloom's taxonomy has driven much of the way thinking has been conceptualized and prioritized. In the original domain of learning "knowledge" (basic facts and concepts and being able to regurgitate them) was at the "bottom" of the hierarchy and "evaluation" (the ability to examine and judge and assign an evaluation) at the top of the learning domain. This hierarchy has been re-conceptualized to place "creating" (the creation of new knowledge/contributing to the field) at the top.

As teachers and parents, we need to offer opportunities for children to engage in all of these cognitive activities. They must learn facts and ideas and get a basic grounding in "knowledge and comprehension" before they can "apply or analyze" these ideas. And certainly they need to be able to pull apart ideas once they have a solid grounding in concepts before they can "synthesize" (put new ideas together and pull them apart) or evaluate them. And as children are often novices in areas of learning, it is rare that they can create and contribute new knowledge, but once they establish a good working understanding and knowledge base and work toward the others—applying, analyzing, and evaluating, then they can be creative and contribute new ideas.

Maslow's Hierarchy of Needs

Before children can engage in really purposeful thinking, they must have their basic needs met. If a child is worried about his or her basic physiological needs or safety needs, then he or she will not be able to engage in higher order critical thinking or problem solving.

We must as parents and teachers make sure that children's needs are met for them to be able to do the challenging cognitive work of purposeful thinking. Once children can engage in more purposeful thinking and mindfulness (as described in the previous chapter) then they can work toward accomplishing that elusive task at the top of Maslow's hierarchy—self-actualization. Our goal for all children and adults is to help them reach their full potential and to feel a sense of self-actualization and happiness.

The Search for Happiness and a Warning

The search for happiness is also elusive, but the one for which nearly all of us strive. Happiness, as Jon Haidt, (2006), in his book, *The Happiness Hypothesis*, argues, based on his examination of the research in psychology, philosophy, and medicine, is based on the following equation:

Happiness = S + C + VS = Set point of happiness which remains pretty constant—it may change temporarily if something really painful and wonderful happens, but the set point theory suggests that we have a set point of happiness that is grounded in our basic temperament and genetics. Some of us are naturally happier than others regardless of life situations.

C = represents the Conditions of our life situation—so the better our life situation—if we have our basic needs met—and our psychological needs met we tend to be happier.

V = represents the Voluntary activities we choose to engage in—that is, what we choose to do that we enjoy/activities that give us pleasure (this is the area over which we exert the most control).

Mihaly Csikszentmihalyi (1990) in his important and groundbreaking work interviewed hundreds of successful people ranging from athletes, painters, and writers, to business people, scientists, and religious leaders. He provided evidence that they all described the time they were most happy and productive in similar ways. He termed this universal experience "Flow." Many might refer to it as "being in the zone." When in a state of "flow" time seems to disappear, you are fully engaged in the now, almost without thought, and your actions just happen without effort. This causes a state of bliss.

Helping children "find their bliss" in healthy expressions and allowing them time to pursue these can go a long way toward increasing happiness. Note, we suggest "healthy expressions"—certainly those that involve hours sitting in front of a television or computer screen playing games or watching mindless television are not healthy expressions—and while children may lose track of space and time and appear to be in a state of flow, rest assured, watching television is not a healthy way to spend one's time and research suggests may actually be counter-productive in building happiness (Kubey, R. & Csikszentmihalyi, 2002).

Recognizing and Representing Types of Thinking

Are there particular kinds of thinking that educators should address more purposefully? As described in the first section of this chapter, we need to cultivate students' ability to think purposefully so they can problem solve and think critically. The following eight forms of cognition/thinking identified in the Thinking Maps theory provide such a model.

Below are the eight forms, which along with metacognition (thinking about thinking) are represented graphically in the Thinking Maps model created by David Hyerle:

1. describing attributes (e.g., describing a character in a story or the characteristics of a science experiment or mathematical formula)
2. comparing and contrasting (e.g., comparing similarities and differences between subplots in a story or two different characters, different properties of matter, or different mathematical calculations)
3. understanding cause and effect (e.g., understanding what caused the Civil War and what some of the effects were or what causes different responses in behavior or science experiments)
4. sequencing (e.g., examining the order of ideas, plots, historical events, recipes)
5. defining in context (e.g., making sense of new ideas by exploring what we already know about them)
6. examining part to whole (e.g., examining parts of the body, parts of a car engine, or parts of a story or equation)
7. making analogies (e.g., understanding the relationships of similar ideas—that is, what common elements make two ideas analogous)

8. classifying (e.g., organizing things into categories—rocks, toys, parts of the brain, chemical elements)

Parents and teachers alike can work with children to build these eight essential cognitive skills, thereby improving children's learning. Sharing these skills with children so that they become aware of their own thinking is also useful for developing young learners. In addition, Hyerle's Thinking Maps provide visual tools representing these essential cognitive skills, which have demonstrated success in improving learning for all types of learners around the world.

While these eight cognitive universals may be activated on a conscious level or purposefully with effort, they are grounded in how, on an unconscious level, the brain learns. That is, neurons in the brain operate sequentially (sequencing) and the structure of the brain is organized in layers hierarchically (categorizing/classifying). New entering information is compared and contrasted against existing patterns of stored information.

New stimuli cause changes to patterns of nerve cell firing, resulting in new learning. The brain interprets qualitative information (qualities) from the senses within a given context and examines the relationships or analogies between what it already knows and what is unknown as it attempts to create its own new ideas using these analogies. Smaller brain structures/parts work together as the parts are greater than the whole. In short, these eight forms of thinking represent how the brain works (Williams & Hyerle, 2010). In a new early childhood program called "Thinking Friends" (Williams, Alper & Hyerle, 2012), barnyard characters represent the eight forms of thinking to introduce children to these different concepts.

What About Children Who Have Trouble with Their Brains and Learning?

Consider the following all-too-familiar example:

> Learning has always been a struggle for me and I have always tried so hard. Sometimes the outcome is good and other times I feel like giving up (College sophomore).

Mel Levine's (2002) work on children with learning differences focuses attention on neurodevelopmental profiles to which teachers and parents alike should be attuned in the growth and development of their children. Parents and teachers are closest to a child's development in these areas, and when any one developmental system (or more) appears to be having difficulty, these adult caregivers should be the first to sound an alarm to get help for the child. Levine is resistant to giving children labels like "ADD" and "autistic";

rather, he discusses each child's unique "neurodevelopmental profile," which might be perfectly suited for school or perhaps something else. He believes understanding the uniqueness of each individual child's mind is healthier than the traditional labels we have come to use in our society for children and disabilities.

He offered the following framework in which, as a teacher or parent, you can pay attention to an individual child's strengths and weaknesses. For example, consider this young woman reflecting on her brother:

> My younger brother has a hard time learning sometimes. He is only in the sixth grade, and is brighter than me (as much as I hate to admit it). He reads novels I can barely understand, and helps me with my homework. Yet, with his ADHD he often struggles, as he is not challenged enough in the classroom (College junior).

Attention Problems

Attention is a complex matter but an essential early step to learning. Without attention, information will not make it into working memory, let alone short-term or long-term memory. As Mel Levine suggested, attention problems are too complex to be lumped into a single "diagnosis" like attention deficit hyperactivity disorder (ADHD), especially when you consider that so many children with attention issues are gifted in other areas, like this young woman's brother, who is very bright linguistically and in other areas of school. Levine suggests that there are several components to attention. For example, a few he describes are

- mental energy controls (e.g., ability to control the level of energy the brain expends on a given task)
- alertness control (e.g., controlling one's level of energy or how awake one is during a learning task)
- sleep arousal control (e.g., ability to control wake-sleep cycles—falling asleep and waking up)
- intake controls (e.g., ability to control information that the brain attends to and takes in)

Levine describes these in greater detail in his book, *A Mind at a Time* (2002). As a teacher or parent or other adult concerned about a child's learning, it is important to be aware of the complexities of attention so that you can get more information and pay attention to the complexities.

Memory Problems

Memory is another complex system according to Levine (2002). True learning (retention and application of information) requires a good short-term, active working, and long-term memory. Levine analyzes the components of memory and describes the ways that learning can break down in each of these places:

- short-term memory (e.g., ability to remember ideas for a short time, like when cramming for a test)
- active working memory (e.g., keeping between five and nine ideas active in one's brain for a short time—such as a telephone number or list of items)
- long-term memory (e.g., ideas that are actually retained and result in a change in the brain); however, one may remember something in long-term memory but have difficulty with the following:
- recalling information from long-term memory
- recognizing an idea or thing that you know in your memory

As adults concerned with a child's learning, we also need to pay attention to memory systems and refer for help when a memory system seems to be breaking down. Memory problems may be masked by other academic deficiencies, so they can be difficult to diagnose. Adults who are knowledgeable about the insidious ways that memory problems can show themselves can be helpful in identifying children with such difficulties.

Many children have difficulty with their language system, which makes it even more difficult or nearly impossible to learn a second language, as is the case with this college student's sister: My sister has had trouble with spelling, and reading. She was in resource classes during elementary and middle school and was evaluated for special education but did not need the services. She is now in high school, in "fundamental" classes. The ranking in our high school is "AP, Enriched, General, Fundamental." Because my sister needed to attend resource classes for reading in middle school, she was not able to take a language. She is now experiencing extreme difficulty in her Spanish class this year.

Language Learning

Levine (2002) breaks down the language system as follows:

- automatic-literate (what we use every day without thinking about it)
- concrete versus abstract
- basic versus higher

- receptive (language we hear or read) versus expressive (language we use ourselves in reading and writing)
- thinking about language (metalinguistics)
- language in big chunks (discourse, or the way we speak, write, or communicate with language)
- words put into sentences (or words in context with correct syntax)
- word meanings (semantics, or what individual words mean)
- word bits (morphemes, or chunks or syllables of words)
- sounds (phonemes, or the sounds of letters)

Language in the form of reading, speaking, and interpreting can be challenging for some children and adolescents. Consider this statement from a preservice teacher candidate in her junior year reflecting on her difficulty reading: It would always take me forever to get my reading done. This would cause me to fall behind in class and I wouldn't be able to participate.

Mathematics/Computational Learning

Mathematics and spatial ordering is another area in which children struggle with learning. Consider this statement from a college junior: I was never good in math and was taken out of the classroom in elementary school for extra help. When I moved up to high school I still had trouble and my teachers instead of helping me made me feel as though I should know the information being taught to me and I was stupid for not knowing it.

Levine examines the complexities of our "spatial ordering system" as well as the "sequential ordering system," both of which encompass mathematical learning as follows:

- spatial ordering system (understanding spatial relations and objects in space, geometry, and so on)
- sequential ordering system (understanding sequences of numbers, order of operations, and so on)

Clearly, children can struggle in one area of mathematics (e.g., computation) but do relatively well in a different area (e.g., geometry) because these skills seem to be handled differently by the brain. Recognizing these as different can be useful in identifying children with mathematical struggles.

Motor Skills and Higher Order Thinking

Some students struggle with their gross motor skills (e.g., running, jumping, hitting a volleyball) and some with their fine motor skills (e.g., writing, cutting with scissors). Levine differentiates also our speaking motor system and our musical motor system (used to play an instrument). Children may struggle in one or more of these areas:

- gross motor (using large muscle groups)
- fine motor (using smaller muscle groups)
- graphomotor (writing)
- oromotor (speaking)
- musical motor (playing an instrument)

Some children struggle with higher forms of learning. Levine outlines the components of the "higher-order thinking system" that encompasses a variety of strategies often used in school and out:

- understanding concepts
- problem solving
- knowing that a problem is a problem
- previewing the outcome
- assessing feasibility
- mobilizing resources
- thinking logically
- considering different strategies and picking the best one
- starting and pacing
- self-monitoring
- dealing with impasses
- arriving at a solution (and checking one's answer)
- critical thinking
- enumerating the facts
- uncovering the author's or creator's point of view
- establishing what one thinks
- searching for errors and exaggerations
- getting outside help
- weighing the evidence
- communicating
- following rules
- creativity
- risk taking
- integrating technical skill with originality
- maintaining autonomy from peer pressures and standards
- suspending self-evaluation
- discovering and pursuing the right medium
- achieving stylistic distinctiveness

Social Skills and the Brain and Mind

Finally, and arguably most important, is our social thinking system. How we interact with others can make the difference between success and failure. As Daniel Goleman discusses in his books, *Emotional Intelligence* and *Social Intelligence*, one's emotional intelligence may be a better predictor of success in life than IQ. Many children struggle with social-relationship building. Adults should help facilitate those relationships and provide tools to children who are struggling. Children with autism or Asperger's syndrome in particular might struggle to read nonverbal/facial cues and need to learn strategies for interpreting the emotions of others. Levine (2002) breaks down what he calls the "social thinking system" for places where problems may occur:

- accomplishing the big three social missions:

    1. friendship mission
    2. political mission (e.g., understanding political relationships in school and out, such as who tends to make decisions in groups, who causes trouble, and so forth)
    3. popularity mission

- social functions and dysfunctions
- expressing accurate feelings
- interpreting the feelings of others accurately
- code switching (e.g., using behavior appropriate in a given setting)
- regulating humor
- developing requesting skills
- mood-matching
- complimenting
- developing lingo fluency
- understanding social behaviors
- resolving conflict
- monitoring one's own behavior and that of others
- self-marketing and image development
- collaborating
- reading and acting on social information (Levine 2002, pp. 60–64, based on Levine's neurodevelopmental model described in-depth in his book, *A Mind at a Time*)

Learning and learning problems are complex, and we as adults need to examine each child and consider his or her unique learning profile. A child may appear to have "attention problems," but this may be a result of a problem with "mental energy control" or "intake control." The bottom line is that we should avoid "lumping" children with learning difficulties into one single category without exploring the complexities of the problem first. More about social relationships and interactions and the important role of emotional states will be discussed in the next chapter.

Interference with Learning: Television and Video Screens

Consider the following examples:

> When I was younger, I had some trouble reading, but got into a reading group before school began and came to love reading. I am 29 and I still love to read books whenever I get a chance to (Graduate student).
>
> We grew up in front of the television. To this day, I am a television junkie. It is very difficult for me to choose to read when the television is on (College junior).

Recently, *Scientific American Mind* published an article titled "Television Is No Mere Metaphor," outlining the ways that television has been found to affect the brain. The authors begin this article with the statement, "Perhaps the most ironic aspect of the struggle for survival is how easily organisms can be harmed by that which they desire" (Kubey and Csikszentmihalyi, 2002, 74). There are numerous issues that parents and teachers alike should attend to when it comes to children's and adolescents' television viewing:

- Addictiveness: Television itself can be addictive in that the brain cannot help but attune to it. The *Scientific American Mind* article reports, "As one might expect, people who were watching TV when we beeped them reported feeling relaxed and passive. The EEG studies similarly showed less mental stimulation, as measured by alpha brain-wave production, during viewing than during reading" (Kubey and Csikszentmihalyi, 2002).

  Also, the brain's "orienting response," which makes us pay attention to something sudden or new, is activated almost constantly during television viewing. Some research has shown that the "orienting response" can be activated as often as once per second—for instance, in the case of music videos. In other experiments where participating families were asked to stop viewing television for a week or a month, many fought more often verbally and physically and dropped out of the studies because they couldn't go that long without watching.

- Computer screens as replacements for televisions. Some children spend as much time, if not more, in front of the computer. Many of the same concerns expressed above apply to children's playing computer games and viewing certain websites.

- Inactivity. Children who sit in front of their computers and televisions for hours a day are not as physically active as those who do not. The brain needs physical activity to produce oxygenated blood cells for healthy functioning.

Kicking the Habit

The authors of the *Scientific American Mind* article make the following recommendations. Individuals or families that want to achieve better control of their TV viewing can try the following strategies:

Raising awareness. As with other dependencies, a first critical step is to become aware of how entrenched the viewing habit has become, how much time it absorbs and how limited the rewards of viewing actually are. One way to do this is to keep a diary for a few days of all programs viewed. The diary entries might rate the quality of the experience, denoting how much the viewer enjoyed or learned from various programs.

Promoting alternative activities. As soon as they finish dinner, many families rush to the television. To supplant viewing with other activities, it may prove helpful to make a list of alternatives and put it on the fridge. Instead of reflexively plopping down in front of the tube, those interested in reducing their viewing can refer to the list.

Exercising willpower. Viewers often know that a particular program or movie-of-the week is not very good within the first few minutes, but instead of switching off the set, they stick with it for the full two hours. It is natural to keep watching to find out what happens next. But once the set is off and people have turned their attention to other things, they rarely care anymore.

Enforcing limits. A kitchen timer can come in handy when setting time limits, especially with video games. When it rings, the kids know to stop. Some parents find that this works much better than announcing the deadline themselves. The kids take the bell more seriously.

Blocking channels/v-chip. Television sets now come equipped with microchips that can be used to prevent viewing of violent shows. In addition, electronic add-on devices can count how many hours each family member has viewed and block access beyond a particular quota.

Viewing selectively. Rather than channel-surf, people can use the television listings ahead of time to choose which programs to watch.

Using the DVR- TIVO. Instead of watching a program, record it for later viewing. Many people never return to much of the material they have taped.

Going cold turkey. Many families have succeeded in reducing viewing by limiting the household to one set and placing it in a remote room of the house or in a closet. Others end their cable subscriptions or jettison the set altogether.

Supporting media education. Schools in Canada and Australia, as well as in an increasing number of states in the United States, now require students to take classes in media education. These sharpen children's ability to analyze what they see and hear and to make more mindful use of TV and other media (Kubey and Csikszentmihalyi, 2002, 80).

Why Read?

Reading is a skill essential to functioning in our society, but it is perhaps one of the most challenging tasks we ask the young brain to learn to do (Sousa, 2006). We are bombarded by print images, and perhaps the most essential skill to functioning well in school is the ability to read. Parents are children's first teachers and need to be vigilant about their child's early literacy development. Teachers pick up the literary "baton" in this relay and help children build their literacy skills. The University of Michigan's Health System synthesized the research on early development of literacy skills has identified five early reading skills that are all essential. They are:

* Phonemic awareness—Being able to hear, identify, and play with individual sounds (phonemes) in spoken words.
* Phonics—Being able to connect the letters of written language with the sounds of spoken language.
* Vocabulary—The words kids need to know to communicate effectively.
* Reading comprehension—Being able to understand and get meaning from what has been read.
* Fluency (oral reading)—Being able to read text accurately and quickly. How can we make reading part of our family's lifestyle? Parents play a critical role in helping their children develop not only the ability to read, but also an enjoyment of reading.
* Turn off the tube. Start by limiting your family's viewing time.
* Teach by example. If you have books, newspapers and magazines around your house, and your child sees you reading, then your child will learn that you value reading. You can't over-estimate the value of modeling.
* Read together. Reading with your child is a great activity. It not only teaches your child that reading is important to you, but it also offers a chance to talk about the book, and often other issues will come up. Books can really open the lines of communication between parent and child.
* Hit the library. Try finding library books about current issues or interests in your family's or child's life, and then reading them together. For example, read a book about going to the dentist prior to your child's next dental exam, or get some books about seashore life after a trip to the coast. If your child is obsessed with dragons, ask your librarian to recommend a good dragon novel for your child. There are many ways to include reading in your child's life, starting in babyhood, and continuing through the teen years. Focus on literacy activities that your child enjoys, so that reading is a treat, not a chore (Boyse, 2008, para. 3–7).

- Encourage play. Play has been found to improve such essential brain functions as self-regulation. As children are spending more and more hours in front of televisions and video games, they have fewer opportunities to practice self-regulation and other imagination-building activities during free play. Also, during free play children are able to practice an important skill called "private speech." We need to encourage children to talk to themselves. In so doing, they learn how to regulate their own language.

WHAT CAN YOU DO RIGHT NOW?

Based on the information presented in this chapter, parents and teachers can do the following to improve learning for children and identify when a child is having difficulty learning:

- Make sure basic needs of children are met and work to improve psychological and self-fulfillment needs and check in regularly by asking "how are you feeling right now?" What could be done to make that better?
- Help children find healthy activities that make them happy and provide time and opportunities to pursue these.
- Help children work on their "habits of mind."
- Recognize the importance of asking the right questions that engage and challenge children at their level.
- Help children engage in problem-solving and the problem solving process
- Become familiar with the eight different types of thinking and help children recognize when these are being used or are needed in learning tasks.
- Help your child pay attention to what he or she is learning in school by connecting the information to areas outside of school. Provide feedback about a child's understanding of concepts.
- Learn about visual tools like Thinking Maps yourself and teach them to your children. These maps have been shown to improve learning for both adults and children.
- Pay attention to neurodevelopmental profiles. Is a child struggling in one or more of these areas? Consult with a pediatrician or other medical professional if necessary.
- Set limits on television and computer game usage, and pay attention to what children are watching.
- Read to and with your child. Encourage reading and build reading skills. If a child is having early reading problems, work with a reading professional and/or pediatrician as early as possible.

- Encourage children to play particularly imaginative games, games with rules and structure, games like Simon Says and Red Light/Green Light that promote self-control, and play involving self-talk.
- Encourage the use of multiple and alternative methods of assessing student cognitive development and learning. Traditional methods of examining student learning (e.g., school report cards and standardized tests) may be inadequate for truly assessing what a child can or cannot do well. Teachers and parents need to be partners in the learning success of children. There are many ways to determine what children know and can do.

The first is to ask children to perform tasks so that you can determine what they can and cannot do or what they do and do not know. One such task is to have children create Thinking Maps so you can determine what they do and do not understand. Observation of children and multiple assessment strategies, such as classroom quizzes, tests, projects, and portfolios, used together can give helpful insight into a child's learning and/or learning struggles.

TIPS FOR TEACHERS

1. Make sure the basic needs of the students in your class are being met.
2. Openly discuss the notion of mindfulness with children and provide opportunities for practicing mindfulness as well as meditation.
3. Consider ways you could build in habits of mind, visual tools, opportunities for and problem solving in creative ways.

REFERENCES

Boyse, Kyla. 2008. Reading and your child. University of Michigan Health System. www.med.umich.edu/1libr/yourchild/reading.htm (accessed August 30, 2008).

Costa, A., & Kallick, B. (n.d.). Describing 16 Habits of Mind. Institute for Habits of Mind. Retrieved June 4, 2013, from www.instituteforhabitsofmind.com/resources.

Csikszentmihalyi, M. (1990). Flow: the psychology of optimal experience. New York: Harper & Row.

Dweck, C. S. (2006). Mindset: the new psychology of success. New York: Random House.

Gardner, H. (2011). Multiple Intelligences: The first thirty years. Harvard Graduate School of Education, Harvard University, Cambridge, MA.

Gardner, H. (2006). Multiple intelligences: New horizons in theory and practice. New York: Basic Books. 2007. Five minds for the future. Cambridge, MA: Harvard Business School Press.

Golman, D. 1995. Emotional intelligence. New York: Bantam Books. 2007. Social intelligence: The new science of human relationships. New York: Bantam Books.

Haidt, J. (2006). The happiness hypothesis: finding modern truth in ancient wisdom. New York: Basic Books.

Hawkins, J., and Blakeslee, S. (2004). On intelligence. New York: Times Books.

Hyerle, D. (2009). Visual tools for transforming information into knowledge (2nd ed.). Thousand Oaks, CA: Corwin Press.

Hyerle, D. (2004). Student successes with thinking maps: School-based research, results, and models for achievement using visual tools. Thousand Oaks, CA: Corwin Press.

Kubey, R., and Csikszentmihalyi M. (2002). Television addiction is no mere metaphor. Scientific American Mind, February. www.sciam.com/article cfm?id=television-addiction-is-n-2002-02 (accessed August 30, 2013).

Kubey, R., & Csikszentmihalyi, M. (2002, February 23). Television Addiction Is No Mere Metaphor: Scientific American. Science News, Articles and Information, Scientific American. Retrieved June 6, 2013 from http://www.scientificamerican.com/article.cfm?id=television-addiction-is-n-2002-02.

Levine, M. D. (2002). A mind at a time. New York: Simon & Schuster.

Pink, D. H. (2010). Drive: the surprising truth about what motivates us. Edinburgh: Canongate.

Sousa, D. (2006). How the brain learns. Thousand Oaks, CA: Corwin Press.

Spiegel, A. 2008. Old-fashioned play builds serious skills. NPR. February 21. www.npr.org/templates/story/story.php?storyId=19212514 (accessed February 21, 2013).

Williams, K., & Hyerle, D. (2011). Teaching and Assessing Thinking to Cultivate 21st Century Skills. Impact on Instructional Improvement, 36(1), 7–15.

Willingham, D. T. (2009). Why don't students like school?: a cognitive scientist answers questions about how the mind works and what it means for the classroom. San Francisco, CA: Jossey-Bass.

Chapter Thirteen

Social Relationships and Healthy Emotions

Our brains are wired to connect. We have mirror neurons in our brains that allow us to experience others' emotions. Interestingly, scientists have shown that mirror neurons are "the neural basis for our ability to understand others' actions" (Thomas, 2012). These neurons show that we are wired to connect and relate. We cry (the only animals to cry tears of pain or joy), seemingly for the sole purpose of showing others our emotions.

Relationships are paramount to our success as a human being. We are social animals that require a level of interconnectedness between ourselves and others. We are born into a type of family unit that may be comprised of a variety of individuals including parents, siblings, grandparents, and other significant individuals. Social ties are important throughout our lifespan from being a child to being an old person.

There is now a strong base of scientific evidence of the positive impact that social connections have not only on our happiness and mental functioning (Five Ways to Wellbeing), but also on a range of other health outcomes (Ryan et al., 2001), and even on how long we live (Seligman, 2011). When children and adults do not have close social ties or emotional bonds, there are more likelinesses of addiction or poor health choices (Dickerson, 2009).

Research has shown that it is the quality of our relationships that have the most impact on our psycho-social development and health. This is influenced by

- Experiencing positive emotions together—e.g. enjoyment, fun
- Being able to talk openly and feel understood
- Giving and receiving of support
- Shared activities and experiences (Maisel, 2009)

It does seem that we are wired for relationships—think of emotions and behaviors such as love, compassion, kindness, gratitude, generosity, smiling, and laughing (Seligman, 2011). Or think about how reluctant we usually are to break bonds with people and how painful it is when we do.

Our need to feel connected to other people—to love and be loved, and to care and be cared for—is a fundamental human need (Deci, 1995). Some experts argue that the capacity to be loved, as well as to love, is the most important human strength (Vaillant, 2008).

In the twenty-first century we are seeing a growth in the number of children who have Reactive Adjustment Disorder, Depression, Anxiety, Social Phobias, School Refusal problems, and a whole level of inability to pursue or maintain healthy social relationships. Our schools are full of children and youths who have been diagnosed or identified as Anti-Social Personality Disorder or Socially Deficit.

NATURE OF THE ISSUE AND HOW IT AFFECTS CHILDREN

Children are now coming to school without the necessary social skills, training, or interpersonal skills that we would see in past generations. These children have not been socially trained through a variety of effective social activities or experiences. Many of these children have been left to their own devices for self-entertainment. Children in the twenty-first century rarely if ever play outside with their neighbors or play at a local park. The social activities usually are comprised of very structured play dates with one other child, or participation on a local sports team, or being part of a dance troupe or playing an instrument through private lessons. There are a growing number of children who are exhibiting severe mental health and social impairment because of the following disorders.

Reactive Attachment Disorder

What is attachment? It is a bond or an emotional connection between the primary caregiver and the infant. The bond affects the child's growth, development, trust, and ability to build relationships. It is a reciprocal relationship and happens after six months of a child's life, but before five years. There are two types: a) secure attachment and b) insecure attachment/attachment disorder which can be inhibited or uninhibited.

Secure attachment occurs when the primary caregiver consistently responds lovingly to the child's needs such as food, shelter, comfort, sleep, and clothing. The infant experiences the emotional essentials from the primary caregiver such as touch, movement, eye contact, and smiles. This builds trust and is a healthy connection.

Insecure or reactive attachment disorder occurs when there are severely confusing, frightening, and isolating emotional experiences in a child's early years of life that disrupt the bond. The following key factors include multiple caregivers, invasive or painful medical procedures, hospitalization, abuse (sexual, physical, neglect), poor prenatal care (alcohol or drug exposure), neurological problems, young or inexperienced mother with poor parenting skills, and frequent moves and/or placements in foster care or institutions. The child learns the world is not a safe place, which results in not trusting, and low confidence. The child now has the belief they are unlovable and will often display similar symptoms of other disorders and may be misdiagnosed with Attention Deficit Disorder, Attention Deficit Hyperactivity Disorder, or Bi-Polar Depression.

The Diagnostic and Statistical Manual of Mental Disorders (DSM-V, 2013) describes "Inhibited Reactive Attachment Disorder as the persistent failure to initiate and respond to most social interactions in a developmentally appropriate way" and "Disinhibited Reactive Attachment Disorder as the display of indiscriminate sociability or a lack of selectivity in the choice of attachment figures (excessive familiarity with relative strangers by making requests and displaying affection)."

Children who experience Reactive Attachment Disorder may exhibit this list of characteristics:

• May be aggressive and acts out because of immature fear, hurt, and anger
• Is excessively clingy and overly demanding
• Lacks social skills
• Suffers anxiety or depression
• Poor eye contact
• Refusal to answer simple questions
• Abnormal eating patterns
• Extreme defiance and control issues
• Developmentally delayed
• Destructiveness to self, others, and property
• Lying about the obvious (crazy lying)
• Stealing
• Absence of guilt or remorse
• Attempts to control attention (usually in a negative way)
• Poor impulse control
• Lacks the sense of right and wrong or cause and effect
• Constant nonsense questions and relentless chatter (Children's Mental Health Disorder Fact Sheet, 2009)

The implications for classroom teachers are numerous in that these early stages of development, that are not adequately developed, create all kinds of challenges for teachers. The lack of adequate or normal experience can result in delays in motor, language, social, and cognitive development.

The child has trouble completing homework, remembering assignments, and has difficulty understanding multiple step assignments. They have problems with comprehension and concentrating. The student has the need to be in control. They show argumentative, defiant behavior, which disrupts the classroom and turns into a power struggle with teachers.

There are some suggested instructional practices that are recommended for this type of student experiencing this level of pathology. To respond with an effective intervention, you need to understand the purpose or function of the behavior. A Functional Behavioral Assessment (FBA) should be considered. Model and teach social skills.

Natural consequences are important. Time-outs do not work. Try "time-ins," which have the child sit alongside of you while you explain how much fun the other children are having. Avoid power struggles with the student. Use humor when appropriate. Do not phrase demands in a question. Allow a response time before repeating the demand. Give choices. Always remain calm and in control of yourself. Make sure to acknowledge good decisions and good behaviors. Instill in the student the understanding that their behavior is their choice.

Classroom accommodations are also needed to help this child be successful. Break down assignments that are difficult. Also help with clarification and multiple-step directions. Being consistent, repetitive, and predictable gives the student the feeling of security and safety, which reduces anxiety and fear.

Create an environment that is highly structured. Set boundaries in the classroom. Be sensitive to changes in schedule, transitions, surprises, and chaotic social situations. Identify a break area or a place the student can go to during times of frustration and anxiety. Make sure it is a supervised location. Set limits to break, such as three minutes or take ten deep breathes (Center for Family Development, 2007).

Anti-Social Personality (Oppositional Defiance) Disorder

Individuals with Antisocial Behavior Disorder or Oppositional Defiance Disorder regularly disregard and violate the rights of others, exhibit aggressive or destructive behaviors, break laws or rules, and act deceitful or steal. There are two types of antisocial behavior: Overt involves acts against people. Covert involves acts against property and/or self-abuse.

Children with Antisocial Behavior Disorder can be identified very accurately at age three or four. There are some very specific symptoms associated with Anti-Social personality disorder: Failure to conform to social norms, deceitfulness, impulsivity, irritability and aggressiveness, reckless disregard, consistent irresponsibility, and lack of remorse.

There is a developmental progression of anti-social personality disorder. At the ages of three–six, we see a series of oppositional symptoms manifest themselves: stubbornness, defies adults, non-compliance, temper tantrums, irritable, argues with adults, blames others, annoys others, spiteful, and angry. At the ages of seven–nine years we see the onset of early conduct disorder symptoms manifesting themselves in the increased severity of the types of behaviors that are now present. We start to observe lying, physical fighting, bullying others, setting fires, swearing, cruelty to animals, and breaking rules. Once puberty and/or adolescence begins, at ages ten–fourteen, we start to see severe conduct disorder types of behavior: cruelty to others, stealing, running away from home, truancy, breaking and entering, and sometimes raping of younger children. Most children diagnosed with Antisocial Behavior Disorder are boys.

Antisocial Behavior Disorder in girls is more often self-directed than outer-directed. Antisocial behavior early in a child's school career is the best indicator of delinquency in adolescence. At least 70 percent of antisocial youth have been arrested at least once within three years of leaving school. Children and youth who are at risk for antisocial behavior patterns are also at risk for academic failure, child abuse and neglect, drug and alcohol involvement, sexually transmitted diseases, accidents, tobacco use, gang membership, and delinquency.

It is unfortunate but the prognosis for these children is not very promising once they have entered the arena of anti-social personality behavior disorders. "Kids with Oppositional Defiance Disorder are essentially handicapped in their ability to be flexible and handle frustration. These kids maintain an oppositional attitude even when it's clearly not in their best interest, so we have to assume they would be doing well if they could, but they lack the capacity for flexibility and frustration management that ordinary children develop" (Ross W. Greene).

Strategies that have been known to be effective in schools with this population are be proactive, redirect, don't take the behavior personally, refuse to join the fight, use simple enforceable consequences, give the child or youth the choices for preferred outcome, and involve and educate parents about consistent practices that can be done at school and at home. Overall, praise the small accomplishments—it begins there.

Conduct Disorders

"Conduct Disorder" is generally used to describe a pattern of repeated and persistent misbehavior. This misbehavior is much worse than would normally be expected in a child of that age. Children and adolescents with this disorder have great difficulty following rules and behaving in a socially acceptable way. They are often viewed by other children, adults, and social agencies as "bad" or delinquent, rather than mentally ill. Terms used to describe the conduct of disordered children and youth are disobedient, anti-social, aggressive, oppositional, defiant, delinquent, and challenging.

The common behaviors are

- Aggressive conduct: Aggression toward people and animals.
- Non-aggressive conduct: Destruction of property.
- Deceitfulness or theft conduct: Deceitfulness, lying, or stealing.
- Serious violations of rules conduct: Violation of parental, societal, or school rules.

Conduct disorders rarely exist by themselves. There is often co-morbidity with the following conditions: Attention Deficit Disorder, Learning, Anxiety, Mood, and Communication Disorders. At times depressive symptoms and alcohol and drug abuse will lead to more acting out behaviors.

Onset of conduct disorders may occur as early as age five or six, but more usually occurs in late childhood or early adolescence; onset after the age of sixteen is rare. It has been shown that when treated, most children and adolescents do not grow up to have behavioral problems or problems with the law. Most youth do well as adults, both socially and occupationally. There are both genetic and environmental components to conduct disorders, which are more common among children of adults with exhibited conduct problems.

Some of the possible causes of conduct disorders are neurological dysregulation, child biological factors, school-related factors, parent psychological factors, divorce, marital distress, marital violence, life stressors, parent and child interactions, and family characteristics. There are five aspects of parenting that are more commonly associated with conduct disorders. They are poor supervision, erratic harsh discipline, parental disharmony, rejections of the child, and low parental involvement in child's activities.

Conduct is usually diagnosed if the following are present:

- There is a repetitive and persistent pattern of behavior where age-appropriate norms or rules are violated.
- Three or more characteristic behaviors have been present during the past twelve months, or one behavior in the last six months.
- Disturbance must cause clinically significant impairment in social, academic, or occupational functioning.

Conduct disordered youth often will manifest neurological patterns of aggression. Over-aroused aggression is aggression resulting from heightened arousal and activity levels, not characterized by intent to inflict pain or by attempts to use aggression for instrumental purposes. Impulsive aggression is aggression that occurs in a sudden burst, without any identifiable precursors or signs.

Affective aggression is also aggression that occurs in a sudden burst, without any identifiable precursors or signs. However, it is aggression arising out of states of intense anger and rage, and includes violent episodes and highly destructive behavior. Predatory aggression is aggression associated with a thought disorder involving paranoia where individuals misinterpret neutral social behavior directed toward them as intentionally harmful. Instrumental aggression is aggression that uses aggressive tactics to maximize an individual's advantage to get their way through intimidation, humiliation, and coercion.

Differences between conduct disordered girls and boys are easily identifiable. Boys are more likely to express their antisocial behavior in confrontational, externalizing forms; girls are more covert and internalizing. Antisocial girls have more psychological symptoms and tend to have higher rates of DSM-V disorders than boys. Antisocial girls also have higher rates of physical, emotional, and sexual abuse. They suffer more neglect, and have increased incidence of family histories of mental illness.

The timing of when the problem behaviors begin will have lasting impact. Early starters are socialized to antisocial behavior from infancy by the family environment and family stressors that disrupt parenting practices. Early starters are substantially more at risk on a host of adjustment problems than late starters. Late starters are socialized to antisocial behavior by peer group influences.

Schools that are more successful with conduct-disordered students are more likely to have structured curriculum and clearly defined expectations. The faculty usually receives professional development and incidents are processed effectively and with a high degree of fidelity of implementation. The programs are challenging yet integrated into the life of the students.

In the last ten years schools have become more aware of how to deal effectively with this type of pathology. Schools have used primary prevention which is an intervention effort designed to keep problems from emerging. Secondary prevention-intervention efforts seek to reverse harm to children and youth who already exhibit the behavioral signs of prior risk exposure. Tertiary prevention-intervention efforts seek to reduce harm for the most severely involved at-risk children and youth.

Parental involvement is a key to effective collaboration between home and school. Parent involvement in the planning and implementation of school interventions is crucial. Many of the adjustment problems that antisocial students experience at school have their origins in the home. The more settings there are in which interventions for antisocial behavior can be implemented, the more likely there is to be a substantive, overall impact on students' total behavior. Parental support in coordinating the school and home components of an intervention can significantly increase the effectiveness of any school intervention.

Parent involvement sometimes opens the door for parent education that can lead to more effective parenting practices, more positive parent-child interactions, and improved student self-esteem. The school can help the parent provide encouragement and discipline at home. Specific skills can be taught to the parent on how to cope with noncompliance, and further education and support can prevent abuse.

There are a variety of effective interventions for conduct disordered children and youth. Most common are behavioral therapy, cognitive behavioral approaches, medication, psychotherapy, and functional family therapy.

Obsessive-Compulsive Disorder

OCD is characterized by recurrent obsessions and/or compulsions that are intense enough to cause severe discomfort. Obsessions are recurrent and persistent thoughts, impulses, or images that are unwanted and cause marked anxiety or stress. Compulsions are repetitive behaviors or rituals (like hand washing, checking something over and over) or mental acts (counting, repeating words silently, avoiding). OCD is a brain disorder and tends to run in the family.

In childhood OCD, a family history of the disorder is more frequent than in adult onset OCD, with genetic factors playing more of a role in childhood OCD. Recent studies have shown that OCD may develop or worsen after a strep infection. Most children go through developmental stages characterized by compulsive behaviors and rituals that are normal—for example, boys thinking girls have "cooties" or collecting things.

Superstitions are forms of "magical thinking" in which children believe in the power of their thoughts or actions to control events in the world. Examples of this would be lucky numbers, or rhymes such as, "Step on a crack, break your momma's back." Normal rituals advance development, enhance socialization, and help children deal with separation anxiety and will disappear with age.

Rituals of the child with OCD persist well into adulthood. They are painful, disabling, and result in feelings of shame and isolation. Attempts to stop doing the rituals result in extreme anxiety. Some of the characteristics that seem to be very common are being overly concerned with dirt or germs (frequent hand washing), long and frequent trips to the bathroom, avoiding playgrounds and messy art projects, especially stickiness.

OCD children have an insistence on having things in a certain order. They have "safe" or "bad numbers" and will often have repeating rituals—for example, going in and out of doors a certain way, taking excessive time to perform tasks, excessive hoarding or collecting, unexplained absences from school, rereading and rewriting; repetitively erasing their work till it often is damaged beyond repair.

Children don't always recognize that they have a problem. Intervention in the form of a combination of medication and cognitive-behavior therapy is often the most effective treatment. Family support and education are also central to the success of the treatments. Medication should only be considered when children are experiencing significant OCD-related impairment or distress. Seven medications make up the first line of defense for OCD. They are Anafranil, Prozac, Zoloft, Paxil, Luvox, Lexapro, and Celexa. It can take up to twelve weeks to determine if medication is going to work.

Cognitive behavioral therapy is another intervention that has proven successful. It is an action-oriented approach to help children confront their fears and learn more appropriate responses to fear-provoking situations. At the same time, a therapist works with the child to limit or even stop the compulsive behaviors that they are exhibiting. Eventually, the child will learn to tolerate disorder without having to resort to compulsive behaviors.

Children are in schools every day so it is important that the educators that work with these OCD children have strategies/interventions. Teachers can be attentive to changes in a student's behavior. They can allow the student to turn in late work for full credit. Educate student's peers about OCD. Post a daily schedule in a highly visible place. Try to redirect student behavior. Try to accommodate situations and behaviors that the student has no control over. Have the student work with a partner so they stay on task. Identify the student's strengths and talents. Be aware of any peer problems or emotional needs of the student. Allow more time for completing tasks and tests.

Children with OCD can be successful in school and in life provided that they are given the right types of support and intervention. One of the major interventions is adult education about the disorder. In that way the adult can be informed about what to do, what to expect, and what to overlook. Awareness of this disorder can create an atmosphere where the student is successful or the obsessive behaviors control the environment and the child and teacher are both unsuccessful at navigating the daily waters of public school education.

Self-Injury, Self-Mutilation

In the last fifteen years a whole new disorder has come to light. Youth are manifesting this pathology in self-injury. This is the intentional, direct injuring of body tissue without suicidal intent. It is an impulsive act to regulate mood. The most common form of self-harm is cutting, but self-harm also covers a wide range of behaviors including burning, sniffing, bruising, scratching, banging or hitting body parts, interfering with wound healing, self-embedding of objects, hair pulling, and the ingestion of toxic substances or objects.

Cutting is often a secretive activity. It is usually done to an area that is easily reached such as the arms, legs, or torsos. It is often concealed by clothing. It is explained away by rational excuses when noticed by others.

The group who is most at risk is primarily adolescent females as well as some males. Youth with a history of sexual abuse or trauma as a child, co-existing psychiatric disorders (addiction, borderline personality disorder, conduct disorder, depression, eating disorders), who lack social support and who lack coping skills and have low self-esteem or a desire to be perfect and have impulse-control issues are excellent candidates.

What are the warning signs? Adults who work with adolescents can be vigilant for the following warning signs: unexplained cuts, associating with peers who cut themselves, signs of depression or poor self-esteem, frequent accidents, changes in eating habits, covering arms, legs, and wrists—even in hot weather—being in frequent possession of weapons or sharp tools.

How prevalent is self-injury? Cutting is the most prevalent form of non-suicidal self-injury. It appears to be increasing in prevalence. In the United States, estimates are 1 in 200 girls between the ages of thirteen and nineteen years old cut themselves! In the past, it was thought that teen girls were more likely to self-injure than boys. Recent studies indicate that the numbers are equal (www.teenhelp.com).

Why do students self-injure? They may lack healthy outlets such as group sports and creative hobbies which help to diffuse tension and stress. Self-injury becomes a maladaptive coping strategy to help a teen release tension and stress through physical relief. Injuring one's self actually releases endorphins, causing temporary relief from emotional pain. One must cut over and over again to get continued relief. It may be a distraction from pain or anger, a way to feel something "real." It is not always the case that they self-injure for extra attention. Many feel shameful about the act and work to conceal the evidence.

Hicks & Hinck, 2009, have formulated best practice intervention for care of clients who self-mutilate. Their intervention has three steps:

1. The provider's self-evaluation of values, beliefs, and assumptions
2. Client assessment
3. Therapeutic strategies (emotional, social, and biological)

Emotional strategies: counseling, journaling, and creative activities to learn how to express feelings safely and productively.

Social strategies: activities to change behavior such as contracts, cognitive therapy, assertiveness training, and problem solving.

Biological strategies: finding natural ways to release endorphins such as exercise. Pharmacological agents may also be used.

What can educators do? Intervene early. Self-mutilators are more receptive to help during the early stages of the disorder. Help students to desensitize to social situations if the cutting is due to social anxiety. Be friendly, patient, positive, and empathetic. Recognize your own prejudices and preconceptions about self-injury.

Be careful not to reinforce cutting by providing extra attention for cutting, but instead try to reinforce positive coping behaviors. Provide opportunities for students to choose assignments that are less likely to produce anxiety. Limit surprises in class by giving students warnings before tests and assignments. Assist with time management for longer assignments and provide support as needed. Recognize that students may experience side effects such as fatigue, weight gain, and inattention on psychiatric medications.

The important things to remember with this group is that self-injury is preventable and with the right type of cognitive restructuring and problem-solving skills these individuals can successfully resolve many of the problems facing them as teens in today's world. It is not hopeless, which is how they often will feel. There are solutions.

Explosive Personality Disorder

Explosive Personality Disorder is an impulse control disorder characterized by episodes of aggressive, destructive behavior resulting in damage to an individual or property. It is also called Intermittent Explosive Disorder (IED). The outburst can occur with little or no provocation. The aggressive, destructive feelings and behavior appear very suddenly and subside almost as quickly. They are often followed by regret or embarrassment over lack of self-control and the resulting damage. The aggressive episodes typically last about twenty minutes and generally occur from one to twenty-five times a month.

Impulsive aggression is a primitive response driven by fear or anger (or a distortion of environmental circumstances) as seen in animal populations. IED and other impulse control issues may be linked in large part to bipolar disorder and serotonin levels in the brain. Explosive Personality Disorder, or IED, tends to be more frequently observed in males than females. Intermittent Explosive Symptoms have been observed in premenstrual women. Between 11 percent and 18 percent of people qualify for the IED diagnosis at some point in their life. The highest prevalence is found to be in younger, less-educated, African-American and Hispanic males. Symptoms are observed to appear an average of six years earlier in males than females (age thirteen as opposed to nineteen).

DSM-V criteria for intermittent explosive disorder:

1. Several discrete episodes of failure to resist aggressive impulses that result in serious assaultive acts or destruction of property.
2. The degree of aggressiveness expressed during the episodes is grossly out of proportion to any psychosocial stressor.
3. The aggressive behaviors are not better accounted for by another mental disorder and are not the direct physiological effect of a substance or general medical condition (From the Diagnostic and Statistical Manual of Mental Disorders, Sixth Edition, Text Revision, 2010, American Psychiatric Association).

The effects on the educator and at school or in the classroom are major. The course of this illness is episodic and unpredictable. It requires the teacher/ aides to establish a rapport with the student. The educator must pick up on antecedents and must have developed a safety plan with the student. Educators must provide a safe environment to handle an episode. Students in class bear witness to these episodes and could suffer lasting traumatic effects.

There is a physical attack with a primary victim, where the student is at the receiving end of the explosive child. There are emotional primary and secondary victims (by-standers) who bear witness to the assaults and are impacted in numerous ways.

There are possible pre-escalation interventions—for instance, during stable functioning the adults can reduce the amount of stimuli on the student. They can regulate the environment to reduce stress, frustration, anger, etc. There can be a reduced emphasis on competition. Teacher and peers can model "socially acceptable" behavior to explosive students.

Educators can provide the student with opportunities for both social and academic success. It is imperative that the teacher have a detailed list of expectations for both the student and other teachers that enter the room or teach that particular group of students. Teachers can also provide ample processing time before transitions, and settle time after a transition. Above all else, the main thing is consistency, consistency, and more consistency.

There are crisis and post-crisis interventions that have proven to be successful as well. Remove the student from the group until they can display appropriate/safe behavior. Treat the student with dignity. Be consistent with consequences. Maintain a "flat affect" when intervening. Intervene early when there is a problem.

Medications and drug treatments specific to IED have not been studied in great depth yet, but a number of medications used to reduce aggression are available. Anti-depressants (i.e., Prozac), mood stabilizers (i.e., Lithium), and anti-psychotic drugs are just several examples. Medications bring out many ethical concerns and may have severe and sometimes lasting side-effects and should be used with caution.

Mean Girl Syndrome

Relational aggression (or covert bullying) "is associated with the formation of social cliques and the subtle and cruel verbal and psychological tactics girls may use to injure another child's feelings of social acceptance (O'Neil, 2008). It includes social isolation or exclusion, exploitation of a friendship or alliance building, manipulative affection, teasing, taunting or insulting, gossiping and spreading rumors, ignoring, staring or giving nasty looks, stealing friends or boyfriends, and Cyber-bullying.

Why do young adolescent females exhibit these types of behavior? The reasons are as individual as the individual girl—it can be out of fear, a need for power and control, social dominance, security, and popularity. Girls learn very young, through adult feedback, to develop interpersonal and social skills, ensure that their interactions have peaceful outcomes, and practice cooperation and communication in play.

Young girls are typically most comfortable playing in pairs or small groups. They quickly learn to "read" their playmates' non-verbal communication, such as intonation, flip of the hair, cock of the head, or body positioning. This sets the foundation for female interactions later in life.

Non-verbal communications can convey an array of messages, and to another girl, can be just as clear as the spoken or written word. They can convey messages such as superiority, power, disdain or disagreement, and covert aggression.

The nature of girls' early friendships may also serve as training for later heterosexual dating relationships: "there is usually an open show of affection between these little girls—both physically in the form of handholding and verbally through 'love notes' that reaffirm how special each is to the other" (Lever, 1976: 484 as cited by O'Neil).

Girls' intimate relationships with their friends often cultivate similar jealousy and possessive feelings commonly associated with immature romantic relationships. Girls' friendships are often dissolved for reasons similar to romantic "break-ups." It often centers around the introduction of a third girl to the relationship that one girl feels threatened by, or a perceived act of disloyalty. Girls often carry this "break-up" mentality to their adolescent or teen relationships, further setting the stage for relational aggression.

The nature of adolescent girls' friendships is quite complex and transitional. Parents are no longer the primary source of social support. The girl begins to rely on peers for social support and values being accepted within a social group. Her peers contribute strongly to self-concept. Female adolescent relationships are generally unstable. Around the age of nine, young girls begin to realize the power they have over the emotions and relationships of others.

Most report the breaking of a friendship as the most anxiety-provoking aspect of school life. A commonly reported reason for the breaking of friendships was the presence of another girl entering, or attempting to enter, into a female relationship being perceived as a threat or breaking trust, such as sharing another's secret.

There exists a hierarchy of power within these adolescent female relationships. Each individual is assigned a role within this existing system or group. The roles are common in that there is the queen, the sidekick, the gossiper, the floater, the torn bystander, "the wannabee" and the target.

The Queen

- Friends do what she wants
- Charming to adults
- Manipulatively affectionate
- Doesn't take responsibility
- Judges peers by loyalty and threat

The Sidekick

- Feels the Queen is the authority
- Gets pushed around by the Queen
- Will lie for the Queen

The Floater

- Moves freely among groups
- Doesn't want to exclude people
- Avoids conflicts
- Higher self-esteem
- Not competitive

The Gossip

- Extremely secretive
- Friends with everyone
- Good communicator
- Seemingly nice and trustworthy
- Uses others' secrets to advantage
- Rarely excluded from the group

Torn Bystander

- Often forced to choose between friends
- Accommodating
- Peacemaker
- Doormat

The Target

- May have fallen from higher rank
- Feels helpless and alone
- Masks hurt feelings
- Feels vulnerable and humiliated
- May try to change to fit in

The "Wannabee"

- Others' opinions and wants dictate
- Desperate to fit in
- Likes "helping" other girls
- Loves to gossip
- Future implications
- Every girl needs . . .
- Social inclusion
- Positive sense of self
- Developing friendships
- Positive communication
- Personal interactions

It is interesting to note that the girls seem to understand their assigned or chosen roles clearly and are often vested in keeping their positions in fear of suddenly falling from grace and becoming the next victim. Research has shown that depending on the role the young female is playing there are serious adjustment consequences that seem to follow.

The bully has some serious adjustment problems such as anxiety and depression, poor relational skills, later delinquent and criminal behavior, early dating, sexuality, victimized, and unplanned pregnancies later in life.

The victim also experiences serious adjustment problems such as anxiety and depression, feelings of loneliness and isolation, poor relational skills, inability to trust, suicide, later delinquent and criminal behavior, sexually victimized and unplanned pregnancies, poor grades, diminished educational experience, distorted sense of self, diminished sense of worth, self-injury, and substance abuse and/or addictions.

The bystanders also experience anxiety, have a diminished educational experience and feelings of guilt or shame for not intervening to rescue or help the victim. All three players in this situation end up losing. They are all victims in one way or another. The ability to be untouched by the mean girl syndrome is very unlikely as it is alive and well in today's schools. Why is this type of pathology so hard to detect? Relational aggression is very hard for an untrained observer to spot. It generally appears to be normal squabbles among girls.

Victims are reluctant to share an incident for many reasons: such as fear of retaliation and further isolation; if it is a friendship "breaking up," she might have feelings of loyalty and hope for it to be repaired. Psychological or emotional abuse is harder to prove and can cause mental doubt and self-blame. Bullies generally focus on an aspect of the victim's appearance or personality. The victim may agree with the bully's criticism, leaving her powerless to complain. Bystanders are generally reluctant to report relational aggression, or to intervene on the victim's behalf out of fear of becoming the next target.

Cyber bullying: cyber bullying fits the nature of girls, and "relational aggression," making it an ever growing tool of choice for girls. The reasons are numerous in that there is anonymity behind a screen name, ability to distance themselves, and feeling less empathy. Lack of rules and regulations indicates a lesser chance of being found out, and fits the covert nature of relational aggression. Social networking and chat rooms play directly to the "mean girls" interest in socially undermining the victim. It is extremely efficient. The bully can spread gossip, rumors, and insults to a greater number people very quickly.

What can schools do? Include "relational aggression" in the school's "anti-bullying policy." Set clear consequences and provide a safe system of reporting acts of bullying. Develop a school-wide understanding of "Relational aggression" and a common language to describe the behaviors. Create a school culture that understands the unstable nature of female relationships, and can identify the difference between developmental friction and unnecessary hurtful acts. Include diversity and empathy training. Create an environment and system where victims can safely receive help.

Schools can use and relate to the numerous resources now available to set policy, and teach awareness, coping skills, and strategies. Practice and teach computer safety. Extend education to parents. Listen, communicate, and observe student interactions. Provide extra-curricular activities that will allow girls to build self-esteem, while getting to know girls outside of their social circles.

This phenomenon will continue to plague our schools unless educators, parents, and community agencies rally to make it unacceptable and provide natural consequences for this type of behavior. There have been instances of mean girl syndrome as early as three to four years old in preschool and in kindergarten classes. We need to get this under control and provide these young females with problem-solving and communication skills so they are better able to navigate their human and personal relationships.

The problems in our schools with children and youth who have some level of deficit or dysfunction are alarming. Educators, parents, and communities need to get on board to begin the collective effort of socialization of our children and all future generations or we will have a collection of anti-social, self-centered, egotistical individuals who are all about the survival of the fittest. It takes a village to raise a healthy, socially competent child.

ONGOING STRATEGIES TO IMPROVE THE ISSUE – HOW CAN WE MAKE IT BETTER?

In the twenty-first century people have discovered that the only way to survive the barrage of stress that bombards us every day is to figure out some level of wellness that allows us to rejuvenate our bodies and our minds. The following are a list of things that both adults and children can do to have a happier life.

10 KEYS TO HAPPIER LIVING (ACTION FOR HAPPINESS.ORG)

1. Do things for others
2. Connect with people
3. Take care of your body
4. Notice the world around you
5. Keep learning new things
6. Have goals to look forward to
7. Find ways to bounce back
8. Take a positive approach
9. Be comfortable with who you are
10. Be part of something bigger

Helping others is not only good for them and a good thing to do, it also makes us happier and healthier too. Giving also connects us to others, creating stronger communities and helping to build a happier society for everyone. And it's not all about money—we can also give our time, ideas, and energy. So if you want to feel good, do good!

No-one's perfect. But so often we compare our insides to other people's outsides. Dwelling on our flaws—what we're not rather than what we've got—makes it much harder to be happy. Learning to accept ourselves, weaknesses and all, and being kinder to ourselves when things go wrong, increases our enjoyment of life, our resilience, and our well-being. It also helps us accept others as they are.

WHAT CAN YOU DO NOW?

Teachers, parents, children, and youth all need to take action towards becoming happier and developing healthy relationships and emotions through the art of positive thinking and a shift in paradigm. Negativity is always with us because it allows us to mobilize into "the fight or flight syndrome," in case of troubling times or events. The art of positive thinking or action is more foreign but very desirable. We like to feel good about ourselves, our lives, our relationships, and our choices.

The following list is not exhaustive but can be done by anyone at any time to increase the likeliness of experiencing success or positive interactions with others or within your school or community. Small things can cause big positive changes, so choose action and make it happen.

1. Thank the people you are grateful for
2. Find three good things every day
3. Look for the good in those around you
4. Bring mindfulness into your day
5. Find your strengths and focus on using them
6. Get help if you are struggling
7. Help kids build emotional resilience
8. Use positive parenting techniques
9. Volunteer your time, energy, skills
10. Help out a friend in need
11. Make something happen for a good cause
12. Make sure to get enough sleep
13. Be curious and get inspired
14. Find your true purpose
15. Give yourself a happiness check-up
16. Learn to meditate
17. Know your thoughts, choose your actions
18. Find your true purpose
19. Really listen to what people are saying
20. Understand each other's needs
21. Get to know your neighbors better
22. Ask others about things that have gone well
23. Get in touch with your spiritual side
24. Detox any negative thinking patterns
25. Get completely absorbed in something

26. Figure out what is important to you
27. Be positive but stay realistic
28. Write down any dreams for the future
29. Be realistic in your reasoning
30. Have happiness on the daily school agenda
31. Boost your positivity ratio
32. Get outside and enjoy the natural world
33. Unplug—take a break from technology
34. Take care of the world around you
35. Find a way to make exercise fun
36. Have tactics for the tough times
37. Enhance your relationships with the people around you every day
38. Make time for fun with family and friends
39. Get a good balance between work and life
40. Create a happier environment at home, school, and work (Action for Happiness.org).

If one was to begin doing all of these suggestions one would have no choice but to have a higher quality of life. Adults must take the responsibility to ensure that the following suggestions are both modeled and enforced with children. Children and youth model what they see in their everyday life. Parents and teachers must be instrumental in showcasing these actions and behaviors on a regular basis so as to provide concrete examples for children to follow.

The following Acronym GREAT DREAM is a wonderful way to have as a daily reminder of what is important in having happy social relationships, mental well-being, and emotional stability.

GIVING	*DIRECTION*
RELATING	RESILIENCE
EXERCISING	EMOTION
APPRECIATING	ACCEPTANCE
TRYING OUT	MEANING
	—(www. Action for Happiness.org)

It is now up to you to begin recognizing and implementing these ideas into your repertoire or skills but even better to begin teaching it to children and youth so that they have a chance at living a quality life and being a fully functional, contributing member of our community.

REFERENCES

Action for Happiness (2013). 10 Keys to Happier Living. Retrieved from www.actionforhappiness.org on September 17, 2013 (2008). Five Ways to Wellbeing. Report prepared by the New Economics Foundation for the UK Government Foresight Project, Mental Capital and Wellbeing.

Center for Family Development (2007). An Overview of Reactive Attachment Disorder for Teachers. Retrieved July 18, 2013, from http://www.center4familydevelop.com/helpteach-rad.htm.

Children's Mental Health Disorder Fact Sheet for the Classroom, 2009. Reactive Attachment Disorder (RAD). Retrieved July 18, 2013, from http://www.ksde.org/KS_SAFE_SCHOOLS_RESOURCE_CENTER/RAD.pdf.

Cutting statistics and self-injury treatment. Retrieved July 3, 2013, from http://www.teenhelp.com/teen-health/cutting-stats-treatment.html.

Deci, E. D. (1995). Why We Do What We Do. NY: Penguin.

Diagnostic and Statistical Manual of Mental Disorder, 5th Edition (2013). American Psychiatric Association Publication, May 27, 2013.

Dickerson, S. S., and Zoccola, P. M. (2009). Towards a biology of social support. In S. J. Lopez, & C. R. Snyder (Eds.). Oxford Handbook of Positive Psychology. NY: Oxford University Press.

Hicks, K., & Hinck, S. (2009). Best-practice intervention for care of clients who self-mutilate. Journal of the American Academy of Nurse Practitioners, 21(8), 430–36, doi:10.1111/j.1745-7599.2009.00426.x. Retrieved July 3, 2013, from Academic Search Premier database.

Maisel, N. C., and Gable, S. L. (2009). For richer . . . in good times . . . and in health: positive processes in relationships. In S. J. Lopez & C. R. Snyder (Eds.). Oxford Handbook of Positive Psychology. NY: Oxford University Press.

O'Neil, S. (2008). Bullying by tween and teen girls: A literature, policy, and resource review. Kookaburra Consulting Inc.

Ryan, R. M. and Deci, E. D. (2001). On happiness and human potentials: A review of research on hedonic and eudaimonic well-being. Annual Review of Psychology, 52, 141–66

Seligman, M. E. P. (2011). Flourish: A visionary new understanding of happiness and well-being. New York: Free Press.

Thomas, B. (2012, November 6). What's So Special about Mirror Neurons? Guest Blog, Scientific American Blog Network.

Vaillant, G. (2008). Spiritual Evolution: How we are wired for faith, hope and love. NY: Broadway Books.

Chapter Fourteen

Strategies for Healthy Well-Being

As you have read this book, we hope that you have been able to develop a new understanding about what it means to be healthy both physically and mentally and how we can teach our children to be mindful and healthy. The pursuit of happiness with oneself and one's life can be hard work depending on the environment or situation in which we may find ourselves. Healthiness and well-being occurs with a concerted effort that is mindful, consistent, and resilient.

Children need positive role models to help them understand and see what it means to be mindful, healthy, and well-balanced. Adults can inadvertently reinforce bad habits, or routines that lead to increased stress and unhealthy patterns of behaviors. The examples provided in this book will hopefully become the status quo and help us as adults be more mindful about how our own behaviors shape those of the impressionable next generation in healthier, less destructive ways.

There are a plethora of strategies that are research based or have extensive personal anecdotes that may confirm that a particular strategy is effective in providing some level of support or benefit for indulging in that strategy. This chapter will provide you with a list of options that you can explore.

HEALTHY EATING STRATEGIES FOR CHILDREN OF ALL AGES

Meals are about more than food. They are a time to connect with your child and support her overall development. Talk with your child during meals and don't let her eat alone. This helps build strong family relationships.

Create routines around mealtime. Routines make children feel loved and secure. They also help children look forward to each meal. You might say a blessing if that's part of your family's tradition. Or, share something about your day before each meal.

Establish regular meal and snack times beginning when your child is nine to twelve months old. Give your child the words he needs to understand the connection between hunger and eating. When your child shows he is hungry, you might say: "You're hungry, aren't you? Well then, it's time to eat!" This helps children learn to link their feelings of hunger with the act of eating at regular times across the day.

Offer three to four healthy food choices at each meal. Research shows that children will choose a healthy diet when they are offered a selection of healthy foods. Don't force your baby or toddler to eat. This often results in children refusing food and eating less. Offer your child a healthy snack between meals if you think she is hungry. This way if she doesn't eat much at one meal, she doesn't have to wait long to eat again.

Limit juice to no more than four ounces a day. Juice has a lot of sugar. And drinking too much juice can fill children up and make them less hungry at mealtimes. Consider adding water to the juice. Offer fresh fruit instead of processed juice.

Be flexible about letting little ones get up from the table when they are done. Babies and toddlers can't sit for long. Plan for three meals a day of about 10–20 minutes each and two to three snacks of about 5–15 minutes.

Don't give up on new foods! Patience is key. You may have to offer your child a new food ten to fifteen times before he will eat it. Encourage your child to touch the new food, lick, and taste it. Let him see you eat it. Children learn by watching and imitating you.

Turn off the TV (computers, and other screens) at mealtime. Mealtime is a time to connect with your child. The television can distract children from eating. It also takes time away from talking as a family (National Center for Infants, Toddlers, and Families, 2013).

It is imperative that children early on develop healthy eating patterns, as it may or may not create a lifelong relationship with food that can become problematic. Parents are the ones who can create that positive or negative relationship with food based on what they chose to enforce or not.

HELPING KIDS REDUCE STRESS

Children primarily learn by example which is why it is key that you provide them with a list of possible solutions for any problematic issues or behaviors that may be creating or causing stress in the child's life or impacting the family life.

The following are guidelines:

1. Eat healthy. A healthy body is better able to withstand stress-induced illness. Schedule regular meals and snack times. Don't allow child to skip meals.
2. Vigorous exercise is a good stress reliever. Just like adults, kids need time to unwind. If kids are bound to video games, television, or a computer, get them on their feet by providing and encouraging the use of active toys like balls, punch bags, and bikes. If the child presently appears to be stressed, make a point of playing with them or take them for a walk. Time spent with kids is a great vehicle for getting them to open up the lines of communication. Walking or hiking out in nature can help reduce stress and allow adults and children quality time to talk and interact about concerns and successes.
3. Be clear in setting rules and consistent with discipline. Kids live in a "black and white" world. Blurred guidelines and inconsistencies are even more confusing for them than they are for adults.
4. Gentle physical touch is a great healer. Sometimes a hug is worth more than a thousand words. Another physical stress reliever can be a gentle massage of your child's neck and shoulders. Like you, your kids can also get knotted up with stress!
5. Learn to be a good listener. When the child wants to talk about his or her problems, don't criticize. In addition, it isn't always necessary to give advice. Sometimes kids just need to talk. Encourage them with open-ended questions like, "So what happened next?" "How do you feel about that?"
6. Teach your kids that everyone (including you) makes mistakes. A good start is admitting your mistakes to your children with an "I'm sorry" or "My mistake" when you goof-up. If the situation warrants, use personal examples of stressful situations you encountered during your childhood. Even if you were unsuccessful in dealing with your situation, you'll teach your kids that you can learn from and even laugh at your own mistakes.
7. Encourage and practice mindfulness. Allow children time to be still and quiet and clear their minds—this could be a quiet walk together or just some quiet time. A time to unplug and clear the mind in more formal meditation or less formal quiet time can help reduce stress and increase the brain's ability to focus attention. Finally, teach your kids stress-relieving exercises and help them find stress-reducing games they can play to reduce their stress (Stress management.com, 2013).

MANAGING FAMILY STRESS

A strong family unit develops the tools to solve stressors, reducing stress for the entire family. When managing individual stressors that affect the family, keep a few tips in mind:

1. Don't avoid discussion. Talk it out and work toward finding a solution.
2. Don't trivialize. Let the individual talk it out, be a good listener, and show them that solving the problem is important to the family.
3. Don't lay blame. When there's a problem it really doesn't matter who's at fault. Define the problem and work toward a solution.
4. Respect privacy. If a family member brings a problem to you in confidence, respect it.

In summary, building a strong family unit that effectively manages day-to-day stressors not only makes your home a place for each member to relax, recharge, and rejuvenate but also builds the skills necessary for the family to come together in a crisis and effectively manage family stress (Stress management.com).

FIVE TIPS FOR A HEALTHY AND HAPPY MIND

1. Meditation/Mindfulness

Research has shown the profound effects that meditation has on the mind, but how many people actually do it on a daily basis? When you meditate, you are giving your mind time to clear, and reformat itself for all the new information that is going to be taken in the following day, or day ahead.

2. Media

The media is very centered on pain and negativity. This fuels pessimism, and ideally it's best to avoid subjecting the mind to it regularly. There is no point in being stressed or worried about something you have limited control over; it's a pointless waste of energy. Beware of brainwashing; all is not necessarily as it seems, and the media are great at exaggerating and bending the truth.

3. Surround yourself with people who give you opportunities to grow

Friendships and relationships are based on love, and love is energy. When the frequencies change, you will find that particular friends and relationships may drop away, or you don't feel you have anything in common with them any longer. If you continue to hold on to relationships which no longer serve you, they sap your energy resources or distract you from focusing your mind. Don't be afraid to let go if you feel the time is right; you will find that new opportunities will arise as a result. You never know who that next amazing person/teacher/friend/lover/mentor is going to be!

4. Eat healthy

Eating healthy and staying hydrated are really important for brain function.

5. Spend your time doing something you LOVE! (And find some physical, cardiovascular activity that you LOVE and do it regularly)

The most important thing of all is to ensure you spend time doing a hobby or activity you love. When we participate in doing something we love, we radiate so many positive emotions, all magnetizing out into the universe to bring you back more joy and happiness. So many people get stuck in a rut and lose focus on what is important and brings them pleasure. Find something you love to do, and do it daily. Make time for it, and even better, make a career out of it! Life is supposed to be an enjoyable experience (Rushforth, 2012).

TEN TIPS FOR A HEALTHY BRAIN

1. Engage Yourself in the Complex and Novel

Learning new information and skills across your entire lifespan helps to keep your brain strong even in the later years of life. Activities that have the highest value for brain health are those that are novel and complex to each particular person. What is easy for one person may be challenging for another, so the things that challenge you the most have the most value for the brain. Therefore, continually learning new things will ensure your brain is always expanding and staying sharp!

2. Exercise Regularly

Exercise has the positive effect of enhancing successful aging. Exercise can improve energy levels, sense of well-being, sleep, and brain health. Engaging in regular exercise also reduces the risk of depression and anxiety.

3. Socialize and Have Fun!

Friends provide opportunities to enable the sharing of experiences, new learning, challenges, emotions, trust, and understanding. Friendship also provides the necessary motivation toward activity and involvement. Engaging in new pursuits with friends often helps develop new life roles, which provide us with an opportunity to feel appreciated, enjoy life, laugh, and have fun. Parent-teacher organizations, churches, sports teams, and other groups and organizations are great places to develop relationships with other people.

4. Be Health Conscious

It is important for us to take control of our health and understand that we are in charge of managing our bodies. We need to have routine medical checkups and have an open relationship with our medical practitioners.

5. Slow Down and Appreciate the Silence — Be More Mindful and Meditative

Society is evolving at an increasing rate, leaving us with little time to relax and process our environment. Our brains require time to process information more deeply, in order to gain more benefit from our daily experiences. The implications of a fast-paced lifestyle are chronic stress and other negative effects on our health and well-being. Reducing demands we place on ourselves is an important step toward stress reduction, and a more fulfilling life. Find time to meditate and be mindful of what is happening in each moment.

A new field of study referred to as neurotheology has been advancing the study of the neurophysiological correlation between prayer and subjective experience. Multiple studies have shown a relationship between spirituality and the immune system. As we continually learn more about the potential of positive thoughts influencing health, people are beginning to integrate these practices more frequently into their daily lives, and experiencing life-changing results.

6. Do Not Retire from Life

Maintaining a strong sense of purpose in life is an important contributor to longevity. Making a conscious decision to stay actively involved in your daily routine is beneficial to your lifelong health and well-being. Positive attitude has been shown to play a significant role in success, as well as your ability to recover from illness.

It is important to develop multiple skills and interests over your lifespan, as we have the ability to learn and develop new talents continually over time. It is our responsibility to nurture different roles and develop personal meaning and life purpose.

7. Reduce and Eliminate Smoking, Drinking, and other Drugs

Mood altering substances, such as drugs and cigarettes, can decrease our functioning, lower our motivation, and impair our cognitive processes. They alter our emotions, which impairs our thinking by reducing focus, attention, memory, and our ability to execute plans.

8. Set Financial Goals

A well-developed plan for financial security is a great way to stimulate your executive functions (responsible for complex activity like organization, scheduling, impulse control, and more). Keeping track of your expenses, and being aware of where your money is going, helps you feel more in control of your financial situation. No matter what expenses you have, set aside 5 percent a month for yourself—you will thank yourself later!

9. Adopt a Nutrient-Rich Diet

Brain-health-promoting-food includes Omega-3 fatty acids found in foods such as fish, flax seed, and nuts. Foods with naturally occurring Vitamin E and Vitamin C have an antioxidant effect. Folate may also help to reduce the risk of some neurodegenerative illnesses and developmental disorders.

10. Maintain Strong Connections

Our ability to communicate and interact with others is critical to maintaining strong connections. Isolation has been shown to reduce our overall health. Research demonstrates the importance of a social network in reducing the risk of dementia. Our ability to continually develop relations and sustain them across our lifespan represents significant health-promoting behaviors, such as stress reduction, new learning, and emotional expression (Nussbaum, P., 2012).

In addition to these ten, we must also get adequate sleep. Different people at different ages need different amounts of sleep. Consistent bed times and wake times have been shown to improve children's academic performance. Also we need to purposefully engage our minds through mindfulness and meditation and improve our attention (control over our brains to do what we wish). We need to also remember that our brains are all wired differently. While we share similarities, the wiring is as unique as our fingerprints. We need to appreciate and embrace these differences.

A quick search on the Internet results in thousands of possible websites that speak to creating a healthy lifestyle for both adults and children. The goal is to help children be mindful of their needs, identify what is challenging or problematic, and consider what needs to be changed in one's daily life to make life better, and actually follow through and do it. Many people spend a lot of time complaining about the woes of their difficult lives yet do nothing to change their life's trajectory. Some do not even acknowledge that they are on a self-destructive path because they are so out of touch with their own minds and behaviors.

Our friends and family are often more aware of our own problematic behavior than we are. This self-destructive behavior often only comes to conscious awareness in an individual's life when it develops into a life-threatening situation. The human brain has a difficult time changing well-established patterns of behavior—even destructive ones, so we tend to deny our problematic behaviors to avoid having to change. The magic of self-awareness through mindfulness is the ability to recognize what is not working in life and change it.

The founders of the "Gross National Happiness Index" in Bhutan have identified key areas found to be associated with happiness:

• Psychological well-being (including life satisfaction, emotional balance, and spirituality)
• Health (mental and physical)
• Education (literacy, knowledge, and values)
• Culture (language, arts, socio-cultural engagement)
• Time management/use (working versus sleeping hours)
• Governance (political participation, political freedom, good government performance and service)
• Community vitality (social support, community relationships, family, support for victims)
• Ecological diversity and resilience (pollution reduction, environmental responsibility, wildlife protection)
• Living standards (household income, assets, housing quality) (From: www.grossnationalhappiness.com)

We must pay attention to a variety of issues like these to truly work on creating a nation that is concerned with raising its "Gross National Happiness Index." Schools and families are positioned to engage children in all of these areas, but only if we are purposeful about it. We can improve the government and the community and the environment if we work together and are motivated to do so to improve the happiness and health of all.

Children and youth need guidance from the adults in their lives to provide them with options and solutions to lead a healthy lifestyle. We all know what is learned in childhood becomes the foundation for future successes or failures. The responsibility lies with the adults. We can start a revolution to improve our Gross International Happiness by starting at home and improving lives in our community and around the world. Healthy brains and minds are an important and necessary place to start.

REFERENCES

National Center for Infants, Toddlers and Families: Healthy Eating Strategies for Young Children, retrieved October 3, 2013, from http://www.zerotothree.org/child-development/health-nutrition/healthy-eating-strategies-for.html.

Nussbaum, P. (2012). Top 10 Tips for a Healthy Brain. *Readers Digest.* retrieved on October 1, 2013, from http://www.rd.com/slideshows/top-10-tips-for-a-healthy-brain-antiaging/#slideshow=slide10.

Rushforth, C. (2012). Mind Body Green. Retrieved October 1, 2013, from http://www.mindbodygreen.com/0-5589/5-Tips-for-a-Happy-Healthy-Mind.html.

Stress Management.com (Stress Reducing Techniques), retrieved October 5, 2013, from http://www.stressmanagementtips.com/kids.htm.

Ura, K., Sabina, A., Zangmo, T., Wangdi, K. (2012). A Short Guide to Gross National Happiness Index. The Center for Bhutan Studies. Retrieved October 4, 2013, from http://www.grossnationalhappiness.com/wp-content/uploads/2012/04/Short-GNH-Index-edited.pdf.

Conclusion

The journey to healthy living and cultivating a healthy mind is a work in progress—one that starts when we are born and doesn't end until we die. We want our children to live long, healthy lives with minds that are as peaceful and happy as they can possibly be. We want to equip our children with strategies and a foundation of healthy habits that become a part of their daily lives.

We all have a set of individual desires that we try to fulfill in a variety of ways. Sometimes we need to find what we really need and differentiate our needs from all the desires we may have on our "bucket list." Maslow was correct in stating that if we don't have our physical needs met we are unable to think beyond meeting those needs. Food and shelter are primary; we spend many hours in the procurement of these things. Once we are beyond meeting those needs we can begin to look more carefully at our drive for self-actualization—what we do and why we do it.

Children have a wonderful adaptability and natural curiosity about life. They are often better able to accept change than many adults because their patterns of thinking and behaving are not as fully ingrained in their brains. Changing well-established habits and life-long routines can be quite painful for many adults who must seek out professional counseling or coaching to begin exploring these unhealthy patterns or behaviors that have controlled or manipulated many of their experiences.

Oftentimes people have not changed these behaviors unless a major crisis, either health or personal, has forced them to re-examine these unhealthy practices. Children unfortunately do not have this life experience or time to analyze the dysfunction and change their behaviors. Adult intervention is the answer to the question of how we can help children lead the healthiest and most emotionally fulfilling lives possible.

As the significant adult, teacher, or parent in a child's life we need to continue to recognize and enhance all of the following qualities in all children:

- Fun seekers: They seek out things that are fun to do, or else they find a way to have fun at what they are doing.
- Attention shifters: They jump from one interest to another.
- Naturally curious: They are curious and usually eager to try anything once.
- Happy: They smile and laugh a lot.
- Emotional: They experience and express emotion freely.
- Creative: They are creative, passionate, and innovative.
- Active: They are physically active.
- Growing: They are constantly growing mentally and physically.
- Risk-takers: They will risk often, not afraid to fail.
- Needy sleepers/resters: They rest when their body tells them to.
- Enthusiastic: They learn enthusiastically.
- Dreamers: They dream and imagine. They believe in the impossible.
- Guilt-free: They don't worry or feel guilty.
- Mindful: They have the capacity to live in the present moment and be mindful of their thoughts and behaviors.
- Empathetic: They have a high capacity for caring and feeling with and about others.
- Kind: They have a high capacity for love and caring for others and the world around them.

Children of all ages have the capacity to achieve all of the possibilities listed above. Adults have to become calculated about making sure that children continue to have experiences that foster the development of the skills that are inherent to childhood.

Healthy and mindful children will create a healthier society that will become more involved in the welfare, supervision, and care of their neighbors locally and globally and the environment in which we all live. Presently the track we are on will result in future generations that are physically unhealthy with large portions of society fighting obesity, mentally unbalanced individuals who are unable to connect and develop social relationships, and an increase in violence and aggression where the amount of murders and physical attacks upon others will become the norm. Gun violence will be the solution rather than negotiation, communication, and problem solving. Is this what we really want for our children and grandchildren?

Every adult who interacts with children is a role model for healthy patterns or actions. We as adults need to lead by example: Robert Cooper summed it up in his book, *The Other 90%*:

Love as if you will live forever,
Work as if you have no need for money,
Dream as if no one can say no,
Have fun as if you never have to grow up,
Sing as if no one else is listening,
Care as if everything depends on your caring,
And raise a banner where a banner never flew. (Robert Cooper)

In conclusion, you can make a difference, one day, one child, and one action at a time. Always believe that every child is worth the time and energy. The time taken to teach a new skill or way of understanding and thinking may have a lifetime of consequences or results for that child before you. Failure is not an option. We cannot afford to lose one of the precious few who are children in the next generation. Believe you can empower every child and troubled youth and you will be successful.

Your role as the adult is to not only set an example as a healthy and mindful person, but to reach out to the children in the next generation to help them become healthy and mindful. Lead by example. Be committed to healthy bodies, healthy minds, and healthy relationships. Help children achieve long healthy lives of meaning and purpose.

54519052R00125

Made in the USA
Lexington, KY
18 August 2016